Heart Washed

A Journey of Grace

ROBBIE BAKER

Published by

Leonine Publishers LLC
Phoenix, Arizona, USA

ISBN-13: 978-1-942190-47-9

Library of Congress Control Number: 2018959580

Printed in the United States of America

10 9 8 7 6 5 4 3 2 1

Visit us online at www.leoninepublishers.com
For more information: info@leoninepublishers.com

TO AUNT CAROL

Table of Contents

Introduction

See, I am sending an angel before you, to
guard you on the way and bring you to
the place I have prepared.
~ *Exodus 23:20*

Brainwashed! I recently heard someone say that my husband, Ken, and I had to have been brainwashed to have converted from our Protestant denomination to the Catholic Church. The truth is that God washed our hearts clean of all the dirt and debris that had accumulated there over the years, then brought us home to the Catholic Church.

I love to read about and hear other peoples' conversion stories; they are such powerful testaments to the fact that God is at work in human lives, bringing us — by whatever means are necessary — to the place He wants us to be. It's easy to think that *we* decided to become Catholic based on *our* studying, *our* thinking. But the truth is, He reduced us to total dependence on Him, to the place where we were finally willing to say, "Lord, I'll follow You anywhere; wherever You take me is where I want to be." We prayed those words with no idea that the "where" would be the Catholic Church.

In the summer of 2004, God took drastic measures with us as He guided our hearts and lives ever closer to His. At that time I would have said that our lives were good, even that we were where God wanted us to be. But as I took an honest look at the relationships I had had in the many churches I had been a part of over the years of my life, I saw a façade of what I had thought it had been. On the surface of those relationships there seemed to be love and joy and peace, but when I looked beneath the surface I saw legalism, judgmentalism, misused authority, and love that was conditional. I felt uneasy and stressed on every level. I remember telling myself, "This must be joy," because the Bible said God gives us joy; "This must be peace," because the Bible said God gives us peace. But in my heart it didn't feel like joy or peace; I didn't feel loved or accepted. I had a very deep love for and trust in my Savior, but at the same time, it seemed to be a somewhat separate thing from the life I was living. It was as if my heart were not in sync with that life, and it did not feel good!

So in that memorable summer, God reached down and plucked us out of our lives. He very graciously left us with our family, our home, and our business, but everything else that made up our life was gone in an instant: our church, our friends, our social activities. We were left bewildered and in pain that was inconceivable to us. We had no one to turn to for explanation, advice, or comfort, except God. We didn't understand that He had put us on a road — admittedly a very long and winding road that led us through the darkest valleys — that would ultimately bring us home to Him and to His Church. And even though my husband and I traveled different roads, we were in the same valley and both roads led us to the Catholic Church.

I am not a theologian, nor can I argue apologetics, but I can share the journey of my heart and I hope that you will be blessed by it.

PART I

Learning to Trust: Conversion

CHAPTER 1

O Love That Wilt Not Let Me Go

THE PAIN WAS EXCRUCIATING. It filled every cell of my body. It filled the air I tried to breathe. It followed me everywhere I went. I couldn't shake it off or run from it. I cried for weeks. I cried while I washed dishes; I cried in the grocery store; I cried in the car; I cried in my sleep. I cried until there were no more tears, then I cried some more. Grief held me a prisoner of paralysis and I would sit in my chair for hours—doing nothing, saying nothing, thinking nothing. I don't remember reading my Bible during those weeks (although I might have). I don't think I even prayed. The pain, the grief, and the loss had sucked everything out of me until there was only a shell left. On the outside life looked almost the same, but on the inside I had died.

There were things in our church that had bothered us from our earliest days there. We had been drawn to that particular church because of its sound doctrine, because of its friendly family atmosphere, and because there were a lot of homeschooling families. We had been homeschooling our children for a number of years and felt certain that we would have a lot in common with those families. We had not been there long, however, when we discovered that we did not: we were not using the "right" home school curriculum; my girls and I wore slacks and jeans; we didn't attend the "preferred" Bible study. The list went on. While these things bothered us, we never really thought about finding another church. We felt like this was where we were supposed to be.

So we tried to settle in and make this our new church home. We eventually began to make friends, got involved in VBS (vacation Bible school), Sunday school, choir, and youth activities, but we never really felt like we belonged. For thirteen years we lived with this uneasiness. When one of our daughters left an abusive marriage, we noticed that people began ignoring us. Only one person asked me how she was doing and there were no offers of help. When her husband eventually divorced her, we discovered what it felt like to be shunned. By then we were hurting and confused. *Was this how Christians were supposed to treat each other?* I felt certain it wasn't.

A few years later another daughter became engaged to a wonderful, godly young man who was a victim of a divorce he didn't instigate or want. We started noticing that our friends didn't seem interested in her wedding plans. No one gave her a bridal shower (in a church where *everyone* gets a big shower). We decided to only invite our closest friends to the wedding, knowing that most of the people there probably wouldn't attend anyway, but only one of our friends came, and that really caught me by surprise.

That was our wake-up call. Did we really want to be associated with this judgmental attitude? Were we becoming this judgmental toward others? (I'm afraid we were.) Were we showing Christ's love in our actions and attitudes? (I'm afraid we weren't.) So when my husband said it was time to leave this church — our home — our whole life — I knew he was right. I'm pretty sure it was the hardest decision we have ever made.

It's easy to think that people leave a church because they are angry about something, or don't like the way something is done, or don't agree with the doctrine. But I can tell you they leave because they are hurting — and hurting badly. When we left this church that had been our home for many years, we did it with extremely heavy hearts, with many regrets, and with sadness beyond words. We had no idea what our future held; we naively thought that we would find another church of similar beliefs, make new friends, and life would resume somewhat as we'd left it.

Toward the end of that memorable summer, we began attending a much larger and more contemporary version of the church we had left. I joined a ladies' Bible study and began singing in the church choir, trying to reclaim my life. My husband and I attended a "community group" with several other couples. We met in a neighbor's home, ate dinner together, and had a Bible study afterward. Although the group fizzled after a few weeks and we didn't connect with most of the people—oh, we tried—we met a couple who would later become extremely close friends and who would help us sort out the recent events in our life.

On Sundays we would go to church, find our seats, try to participate in the service, then make our way back to the car for the trip home—all without any human interaction. We were completely alone in the midst of hundreds of people. Every Sunday for a year I cried all the way home from church. Deep in my heart I knew this wasn't where we belonged.

At the local university that fall, I sang in a choir that rehearsed three afternoons every week. As I look back, I can see how desperately I was trying to recreate something that resembled my life. I now see that I tried too hard; I did too much. When I was a part of that choir, I got to know quite a few students who were here from almost every part of the world; I heard their stories and listened to their hopes and dreams. When I asked them how things were going and they burst into tears, I knew we'd be sitting on the sofa in the third-floor hallway for a good long while. With these kids I was able to reach past my own pain and numbness and touch their lives in some small way. They accepted me just the way I was, and I realized I could be completely myself with them. My husband kept telling me I needed some grown-up girlfriends, but I think for that time, those precious young people were exactly what I needed.

It took me a long time to understand that life's hard trials are actually God's mercy and compassion in action. They can be painful and sorrowful, but if we let them, they bring us closer to Him. He is always there to comfort us, to guide us, to hold us up when we fall, to carry us when we can't walk, to tenderly dry our tears, but we still must walk through the dark valleys. When we can gain some perspective, we begin to understand that there *is* the other side and that we *will* eventually be there. Our hearts will be cleaner, our spirits will be stronger, and we will be more of what Christ wants us to be. We can leave a little more of "us" behind and become more like our Savior.

CHAPTER 2

Great Is Thy Faithfulness

*T*HINGS GOT WORSE. MUCH WORSE. In the middle of the following spring I experienced a personal crisis that took me all the way to the bottom of a deep, dark pit. Even today only two other people know of that crisis and the deep, deep despair I felt. I couldn't talk to my family and I had no friends to turn to. My entire life was crumbling around me and I was completely alone. I didn't feel abandoned by God during that time, but it was as if He were very, very distant. I tried to reach out for Him, but I couldn't touch Him. God was at work laying the stepping stones for my healing and my life, but in my grief I couldn't see that yet. I couldn't feel His presence. All I could feel were pain and despair and hopelessness.

In January a new adult chorale was formed at the university and I couldn't sign up fast enough. (You might have guessed by now that singing is a very important part of my life. I'm convinced that it is one of God's best therapies.) Great people joined this choir and several of them played significant roles in my healing process. A young man we had met at the university the previous year also joined the chorale. He was walking me to my car after a rehearsal one night and asked what was wrong, that I just didn't seem myself. I couldn't share the details of my despair (poor guy—that would have been the end of our friendship), so I just said that I was having a really hard week. His response was, "I'm sorry you're hurting. Is there anything I can do?"

"I'm sorry you're hurting." Those were the most amazing words I had ever heard! I don't think anyone had ever cared whether or not I was hurting, much less felt any sorrow over it. "Is there anything I can do?" These words, this caring about *me*—as opposed to my *behavior*—were balm to my soul. They oozed over me and covered every sliver of pain. They changed my heart forever. That young man doesn't know that he was an angel sent to me by God that night. I am so thankful for the lessons he taught me: lessons about treating people—all people—with dignity, respect, and genuine caring; lessons about compassion and gentleness and real friendship.

The following day after an afternoon choir rehearsal (I was still trying to do too much), I was getting off the elevator in the parking deck and ran into a lady I had met the previous fall in the music building. We had visited a number of times and had shared some personal parts of our lives, so she knew that something was terribly wrong when she saw me. She hugged me and the tears came. Bless her heart—she stood there by the elevators, kids constantly coming and going around us, and hugged me and cried with me for over an hour. She didn't ask me what was wrong; she didn't offer advice; she simply shared my pain. What power we have in peoples' lives when we're willing to put ourselves aside and just be there for them in their lowest, weakest moments!

Later that week the neighbor that I had met at our community group Bible study the previous fall called to see if I wanted to go for a walk with her. We had been getting to know each other over the winter but our friendship was still in its early, testing-the-waters stage. We had both learned to choose our closest friends wisely and carefully, and we didn't know for certain where our friendship was headed. We were at the park walking her two little dogs when she, too, asked me what was wrong. I told her I was going through a crisis and didn't know if the outcome could ever be anything but disastrous; I didn't know what to do. And then more amazing words: "Do you want to talk about it?"

"Like I talk, then you tell me what to do? Like I talk, and you explain to me how I got into this mess?

Like I talk, and you decide you can't be my friend because of the mess I'm in?"

"No. Just talk."

So for the first time I had someone to talk to, to share what had happened, to share the current circumstances of my life. And do you know what? She listened—really listened. She asked what I thought about all the events and people that had been instrumental in my being in the situation I was in. She shared some situations in her own life that had been similar. I asked her how she had healed and she shared what she had learned, but never in an "I'll teach you the lessons you need to learn" way. That afternoon was the beginning of one of the best friendships God has ever given me. *What a wonderful gift!*

In the deepest recesses of my soul, God's strength was sure. I couldn't feel it and I wasn't even aware of its presence, but it was there nonetheless. As I look back on this period of my life, I can see that we can't depend on our feelings to tell us the truth of the reality taking place. Our feelings are subject to the whims of our past and current circumstances; they can take us from the highest highs to the lowest lows in seconds. But God is constant—His presence, His comfort, His strength. In the deepest currents of my life God was sustaining me. Even though I couldn't see the outcome, He could, and my spirit recognized this in spite of my outward despair. He sent just the right people at just the right times to give me what I needed to keep going. It would have been so easy for me to give up, to decide that God wasn't the loving, caring God I had known Him to be. But His strength steadied me, and I was reminded by these three special people that He was at work — beyond my sight, beyond my feelings — quietly and steadily moving me forward to the place He had prepared for me. And within parts of me I couldn't reach, I knew that it would be worth any amount of suffering to be with my Savior for all eternity.

CHAPTER 3

I Saw Jesus In You

❋

I MET AUNT CAROL IN JUNE—exactly one year into my journey. She had just had surgery. She had been diagnosed with cancer and told she had only a few months to live. She was pretty spunky to be that sick. I loved her on sight. We didn't visit long, but she told me that she was ready to face her Maker, ready to leave this life behind her. And yet there was a twinkle in her eye, a joy that surprised me. I left her hospital room that day telling myself that it was a shame she wasn't *really* saved, because I knew she was a Catholic and Catholics weren't *really* Christians. But somehow, deep in my heart, that didn't ring true. My past teaching and the reality in front of me simply didn't match.

Whenever I would think back on that sunny summer day and the very special lady in that hospital room, memories from my teenage years began to haunt me. I remember hearing stories about and seeing pictures of Rose Kennedy burying her sons.

The media told story after story of the tragedies in her life. When they asked her how she could survive so many tragedies, she always answered, "My faith is what gives me strength." Of course, I *knew* she wasn't a Christian because she was a Catholic. (The things we hear as children sink in and keep us hostage until we are able to step back and look at situations without prejudice. But I was still too young to be able to do that. It would be many more years before I could.) I didn't really know what she *did* when she went to daily Mass, but I was sure it wasn't good. And still, deep down, I wondered how she could talk about her faith, how she could keep going amidst such tragic circumstances and not be truly saved. I tried to bury those thoughts, but every so often they would surface to bother me. They were bothering me now.

A picture turned my world upside down. It had been taken a few weeks after that first visit in Aunt Carol's hospital room. She was very ill and weak and leaning on the arm of a handsome young man. It looked as if she were totally dependent on his strength to get her through the day — the day of her son and daughter-in-law's wedding. What you wouldn't know just by looking at the picture was that she was leaning on the arm of her other son's partner. She treated him with the same dignity, respect, care, and unconditional love that she treated everyone with. And then I realized what I was *really* seeing: I was seeing God's love! The realization hit me — quite forcefully — that I had never really seen Christ's love in action before. Scripture tells us that Christ loved us, Christ died for us "while we were yet sinners" (Romans 5:8). And the only Catholic I knew was showing me what that love looked like.

My world stopped spinning that day. I was stunned and completely shaken. If Catholics weren't *really* saved, how could they possibly be the ones showing the world what God's love looks like? I had to leave all my preconceived ideas behind me and look at Catholicism honestly for what it was (at least the part I was seeing). That was all I could think about for weeks, but I was still very far from thinking about *being* a Catholic.

Aunt Carol suffered her last months with a dignity and trust I had seen only one other time in my life. I never heard her complain or wish things were different; she simply accepted her circumstances as God's plan for her life. She still glowed with joy and courage and peace. She had chosen a quote from Saint John of the Cross to put on the programs for her memorial service a few months later. "And I saw the river over which every soul must pass to reach the kingdom of heaven. And the name of that river was Suffering. And I saw the boat which carried souls across the river. And the name of that boat was Love."

She never did anything intentionally to change my life; she just lived her life as close to God as she could and let Him use it to touch others. Sometimes we think we need to save the world, yet God has called us to live holy and godly lives, to reach out and love and care for other people in the same way He loves and cares for us. Sometimes when we try to talk to people about "being saved," our words get in the way, or the way we live gets in the way of our words, and we end up causing hurt and harm instead of love and care. Aunt Carol showed me that people take notice when you radiate joy in this world, especially when that joy shines in the midst of hardship and suffering. And such joy can only come from being right in the center of God's will for us, from being exactly where He wants us to be, from trusting Him completely with the circumstances of our lives.

CHAPTER 4

Be Still My Soul

IKE THE ISRAELITES IN THE DESERT, always looking at what they had left behind in Egypt and longing to go back, I kept looking at everything I had lost in my life and trying to get at least some of it back. I kept thinking how silly, how stupid those Israelites were. Couldn't they see that God had something better waiting for them? Could they only remember the few good things about being slaves in Egypt? I slowly came to realize that I was guilty of doing the same thing; I kept trying to recreate my old life instead of looking forward to a new one. To give myself and those Israelites some credit, when it's all you've ever known, it feels as if that's all there is. We can only see, can only feel the here and now, and we forget that our great God sees the entire picture—from eternity to eternity. When things don't seem to be going well, we tend to see only the circumstances that brought us here. For weeks I pondered the idea that I *was* trying to recreate my old life. But what was the alternative? I didn't know.

Then one day it happened. I hesitate to call it a vision, but I'm not sure what else I *could* call it. I was in my car driving home one afternoon, and as I pulled up to the stop sign near my neighborhood I saw a clear picture of God's mighty arm coming down from heaven and sweeping everything off the entire length of the long table of my life. Everything crashed to the floor in a pile of rubble. As I looked at the shattered remains on the floor and the empty table, I realized for the first time that God does not clear the slate unless He has something better to give us. I was stunned. God was clearly showing me that He had something for me that was so much better than anything I had ever had before, but I simply couldn't imagine what it could be. We had visited every "Bible-believing" church in our area, and whatever God had for us was clearly not to be found in any of them. My mind and my imagination had nowhere else to go; I was feeling caught in a twilight zone. The reality in front of me just wasn't making sense, but I knew there was something else out there that I couldn't quite grasp.

Sometime during that summer, we made the decision to stop going to church anywhere. We were so miserable where we had been going, and we felt as though there weren't any other options. We also began to feel that no church was better than a church where Christ's love was inaccurately represented.

An interesting by-product of that decision was that I began reading my Bible again. Voraciously. I read it from cover to cover. I found different topics to study. My first topic was, "What does the Bible say about how we are supposed to love other people?" I don't think I learned anything I didn't already know, but it was good to gather it all in one place and ponder it. Jesus tells us to love others "As I have loved you" (John 13:34). How has Jesus loved me? He laid down His life for me (John 15:13), and He did it while I was still a sinner (Romans 5:8). He loves me with "enduring love" (Isaiah 54:8). That's beyond my comprehension, yet He tells me that I'm supposed to love other people in the same way. I learned that love builds people up (1 Corinthians 8:1); love serves people (Galatians 5:13); love "bears one another's burdens" (Galatians 6:2); love is "kind...love endures all things" (1 Corinthians 13:4, 7). I don't think I had ever witnessed that kind of love — parts of it certainly, but never all of it — except in a little, dying, Catholic lady I had recently met.

My next question was: "What has Christ done for me?" I found that He is always with me (Matthew 28:20). Always! That means He is with me now, even in the midst of all this uncertainty, this pain, this confusion. "Always" means He will never leave me. He made me a child of God (John 1:12).

I am a child of God! I thought about how much I love my own children and how I would do anything within my power to give them the best I have to give. If God loves me like that then He must want to give me the best He has to give, and since He is the great God of the universe, His best *is* the best there is! He's given me eternal life, life with Him forever (John 3:36). He's given me His grace, and it's sufficient (2 Corinthians 12:9). Sufficient for today. Sufficient for tomorrow. It's enough. It's all I need. As I read, studied, and pondered these verses, for the first time in a long while I felt the stirrings of life awakening deep within my soul. I couldn't see where God was taking me, but I finally had a strong sense that He was on this journey with me, leading the way, preparing me for something new and wonderful. The hurt, the pain, and the confusion were still with me, but deeper than all those, I knew with certainty that my wonderful Savior was also still very much with me.

A few weeks later, I was reading a book that a friend had recommended, and I came across a passage that stopped me in my tracks. The writer was discussing spiritual "rules": "love God," "love your neighbor," "forgive your enemies," "be righteous," "be holy," and how our human nature wants to "try harder" to do and be those things God asks us to do and be.[1] We wear ourselves out and burn ourselves out by continuing to work harder. Instead, we need to "rest again in the performance of Christ, on the cross for life, and through His Spirit for living."[2] The right response is to "fall on our face in the presence of God's perfect grace and say, 'I can't do it. I need a gift.'"[3] The Bible says that the kingdom of God belongs to broken people, people who are poor in Spirit (Matthew 5:3). For the first time in my life I felt I understood what that meant; I felt broken and poor. For the first time in my life I quit trying to do everything myself. I was finally able to rest, to be, and to stop doing.

I remember having discussions with people about how we are supposed "to rest" in Christ. The answer always seemed so elusive, yet here it was and it was so simple. Not necessarily easy, but simple. Just respond to God with the plea, "Lord, I can't do what you want me to do. Please do it for me!" What freedom! I could finally quit trying and let God do it for me. The confusion of trying to understand everything that had happened to us, of trying to figure out what we were supposed to be doing and where we were supposed to be doing it,

---

1   David Johnson and Jeff Van Vonderen, *The Subtle Power of Spiritual Abuse* (Bloomington, MI: Bethany House Publishers, 1991), 85.

2   Ibid., 85.

3   Ibid., 96.

of trying to reclaim our lives—I gave it all to God and asked Him to take care of it for me. I was so very tired from carrying the load, and all along He was there, wanting to carry it for me. And truly, it felt as if the weight of the world was lifted from my shoulders, and I could finally just *be*.

CHAPTER 5

Be Still and Know That I Am God

*I*WAS IN CHILI'S EATING MY LETTUCE WRAPS when my friend challenged me: Could we look for the hand of God in our lives every day, then journal where we had seen Him at work? No matter how hard it was or how insignificant it seemed, we would write something every day. Some days it was almost impossible to find something to write; some days it was so easy to write.

Once I was frustrated by a delay getting out the door and then came upon a serious accident on the road that had just happened. Had God spared me? Or extra money came in the mail from an unexpected source that was just enough to cover a bill we hadn't anticipated. A gift from God? I nearly cut my finger fixing dinner, but I didn't. I happened to have some odd thing in the house one of the kids needed to borrow. I had a quiet day just to read and relax. Were these small things also God working in my life? It didn't really feel like it at first, but the more I practiced looking, the easier it was to see Him there — in the big things *and* the small.

The external voices were gone from my life and I was getting reacquainted with the voice of the Holy Spirit. I hadn't realized that His voice had been drowned out by the many voices surrounding me, telling me what the Bible says or means, what I should do in whatever situation I found myself at the moment, what I should be learning from the current circumstances of my life. These voices had become loud and insistent, but the one voice I needed to hear was still and quiet.

As I read my Bible that summer, as I pondered verses that spoke to me, as I settled into "being," that still, small voice gained strength and it became easier for me to hear Him. At the same time, like two sides of a coin, it became easier to talk to Him, to pour out my pain and confusion. And over the course of the summer, He replaced the pain and confusion with happiness. It wasn't quite peace, but I definitely felt more settled than I ever had. I remember thinking how odd that was because, outwardly, nothing seemed to be falling into place. We still had only one couple for friends; we still weren't attending a church anywhere; we still felt as if we were living borrowed lives. It wasn't quite joy, but I felt more contentment that I ever had. That also seemed odd, because there was nothing about my life just then that seemed especially right.

The more I was able to see God in my life, the more I was able to hear His voice, to rest and simply "be," the more I was able to trust, to hope, to wait. And as I waited, God began to give me strength, courage, and comfort. I'm not sure I actually felt those things, but they were becoming visible to the people closest to me. One day I was in the grocery store and ran into someone whom I hadn't seen in over a year. She said, "You seem different." And my response was, "I'm happy." The thrill of saying those simple words—and meaning them—caught me by surprise and lifted me up to a place I hadn't been in a very long while. God had definitely been working!

Still, I wasn't living in such a place all by myself. My husband and I had just walked in the door with our suitcases, exhausted from travel and jetlag. We had hardly set our things down when one of our daughters told us that she was going to become Catholic. We were taken totally by surprise. She said that she had been asking a lot of questions (she had found a Catholic website) and studying a lot of Scripture and felt that she was doing what she needed to do. I can't say that I was happy about it, but her mind was made up and she was, after all, an adult. At the same time that we were having our crisis, she was having a crisis of her own. And so were most of our children. They had been suffering the same pain and confusion that we had been and were traveling their own roads in the valley. They were struggling to free themselves from their past, too, and were trying to find their own relationships with their Savior. As parents we needed to give them the freedom and the space to do that, then respect their choices, even if they weren't the choices we would make.

I find it interesting that as I look back on that time, I made no connection between the Catholic lady I had met and our daughter's decision to become Catholic. These events seemed completely unrelated. God was working, but this time I missed it! As our daughter studied and went through RCIA (Rite of Christian Initiation of Adults) classes, I remember asking her questions, but it was only intellectual curiosity on my part. I *certainly* had no intention of *ever* becoming Catholic!

God must have been in heaven, shaking His head at my density. I was completely alone and lost in the valley, with nowhere to call home, and when He gave me glimpses of that home, I told Him I was sure He'd never take me *there*. As we walked that road together, hand in hand, He always walked with me at my pace, and when I needed to back up a few steps or just stop to rest and absorb what I was learning, He patiently stopped and waited with me. He never rushed me, He never coerced me; He simply invited me to follow Him in love. As we walked together, God's healing was taking place in my heart. I couldn't see it, but slowly, little by little, I was gaining strength, the wounds were beginning to heal, and I was getting closer to my new home.

Sometimes I feel as if God isn't working in my life; I feel as if He's very far away. But as I've come to learn, it isn't that He's not here and working, it's that I'm too busy or too stubborn to see Him. I need to learn to let go of so much busyness and stuff and learn to spend time quietly with Him. As I was learning that summer, we don't always need to be praying or meditating or reading our Bibles (although those are all certainly necessary). Sometimes we can just sit and *be* with our precious Savior. And while we are not doing, He is. He can accomplish more in our souls in those quiet times than we can accomplish in a lifetime of prayer and meditating and reading. He will surely come when we ask Him in. He will surely walk the lonely road with us, and He will surely bring us home when we are willing to follow Him in complete trust. And when we stop telling God Almighty what we think He wants us to do, we will finally be where He wants us to be.

CHAPTER 6

Wonderful Grace of Jesus

❀

THE FOLLOWING MONTHS were a study in God's overwhelming grace. As I look back over the calendar for that time, I can only wonder how we survived all the crises that came our way. Yet I don't need to wonder for long, because I know it could only have been God's grace, given to us moment by moment as we needed it.

It was a season of near disasters of one sort or another: passports lost in Hurricane Katrina; Hurricane Rita hitting Houston where a daughter lived; several deaths in our extended family; my husband's bout with a couple of serious illnesses; my own share of sickness; a grandchild near death at one point; a son joining the Army and heading for Iraq. It's good that these things happen to us mostly one at a time, and God gives us just the right amount of grace for each one as it comes. If we could see the crises coming, we would be so completely overwhelmed that we wouldn't be able to face them.

But God knows that, and He sends what we can bear with His loving and merciful grace.

I'm reminded of a song that I love and wish we sang more often: "He Giveth More Grace," written by Annie Flint and Hubert Mitchell early in the twentieth century.

> *He giveth more grace when the*
> *   burdens grow greater;*
> *He sendeth more strength when*
> *   the labors increase.*
> *To added affliction He added His mercy;*
> *To multiplied trials, His multiplied peace.*
> *When we have exhausted our*
> *   store of endurance,*
> *When our strength has failed*
> *   ere the day is half done,*
> *When we reach the end of our*
> *   hoarded resources*
> *Our Father's full giving is only begun.*
> *His love has no limit;*
> *His grace has no measure;*
> *His power has no boundary*
> *   known unto men*
> *For out of His infinite riches in Jesus,*
> *He giveth, and giveth, and giveth again!*

"When we reach the end of our hoarded resources..." Why do we think we can do anything by our own efforts? Why do we think *we* can fill our tanks with the necessary reserves to take us through the rough patches of our lives? It's only when we run out of our own abilities that we give God the room to give us what we need. And then He gives us so much more.

During this fall and spring, it seemed as if there wasn't anything really happening spiritually, but God was laying the groundwork, preparing us for the final leg of our journey home. In spite of the outward craziness of our lives, there was an inward settledness that only God could give: the ability to rest and "be" in the middle of busyness and uncertainty, and increasing trust as we gave each moment to our Savior to do with as He willed. Our strength was growing, and with it the beginning of hope.

On Christmas Eve of that winter, we went to our first Mass. We sat timidly in the back row, certain that we would hear heresy. Over the course of that spring and summer, we attended Mass with our daughter a few more times. I listened to everything with a critical ear, but, to my surprise, I didn't hear anything heretical. There was certainly plenty that I didn't understand: holy water, genuflecting, what the priests were doing at the altar; but what I *did* see were humble and kind people who reminded me of my Catholic friend who had recently died. Were all Catholics like that? I'd have to think on that one for quite a few more months!

I was also quite impressed with the amount of Scripture that was read and sung, and I was beginning to be drawn to the personal participation that was a large part of the Mass. I actually got to sing "Holy, Holy" and "Glory to God" every Sunday. But I think what really soaked in and wooed my soul was saying, "Lord, I am not worthy that you should enter under my roof, but only say the word and my soul shall be healed" (taken from the words of the centurion in Matthew 8:8). Over the course of our visits, those words began the healing of my spirit, the healing of my mind, the healing of my heart. They soaked deep into my soul and stayed there.

When life is busy we're all too aware of the events themselves, but it takes quiet times with our Lord to begin to see His hand at work beneath the surface. As I look back on those crazy, stressful months, I can see God's grace at every turn; I can see how He gently introduced us to His Church; and I can see how He used the liturgy to accelerate my healing. Although I still believed I would never be a Catholic, God was slowly but surely drawing me closer. When I entered the church there was a tangible, cool, peaceful Presence that, at that time, I couldn't identify. Yet that Presence tugged on my soul, healed my heart, and gave me new hope for my future.

CHAPTER 7

Jesus, Lover of My Soul

T WAS EARLY IN THE SUMMER OF 2006 that I dared to dream again. I finally had the hope of discovering my identity (it was devastating to realize I had lost it), of becoming the person God meant me to be, of making my life something to be embraced and cherished. That's one thing about having everything taken away — there is nothing left to lose and everything to gain. I'm reminded of a verse that says it all: "For whoever wishes to save his life will lose it, but whoever loses his life for my sake will find it" (Matthew 16:25). I didn't know then how close I was to finding it.

I began to get reacquainted with myself in what seemed like a very non-spiritual way. I was getting ready to decorate our house, and I wanted it to reflect the personalities of our family, to be a place that feeds and nurtures us emotionally, a place where guests would find God's love and peace. In order to do this I tried to think of ten words that define me (a hard task for someone who has no clue who she is). After much prayer and contemplation, I came up with a list that surprised me.

The first word was easy: music. Music expresses my soul even when no words can. Music feeds my soul and restores my equilibrium when things are off-kilter. The second word was family. No surprise! My family is my joy. Sunshine was third. Sunshine gives me energy and passion. Next was beach. I love the feel of sand between my toes; I love to hear the waves crashing against the shore; I love to see the sunlight dancing on the water; I love to watch the sunset with someone I love; I love the feel of icy water on my skin. Richness was fifth. Rich colors and textures represent depth and richness of life. And space: physical and mental space to be quiet and to think things through. Seventh was beauty. God created a beautiful world and I wanted my surroundings to reflect my God. Next was home. Home is the one place on earth where I can completely express myself, a place that nourishes me, a place full of people I love, a place to share with friends, the center of my world. Number nine was creativity. I *need* to create things: making something brings me deep satisfaction. And last on the list was contentment. Hmm…I am content with what God has given me: a husband I adore, wonderful children I am so proud of, precious grandchildren that brighten my days, a beautiful home, my mom living close by, a great choir to sing with, peace in my soul.

I decided that these ten words really did describe me. I had finally given myself permission to be myself instead of trying to be what other people thought I should be. Having a good sense of who I really was provided the shot of adrenaline I needed to finally move forward.

We were beginning to feel that if we could find a church that felt like home and make some new friends, life would be complete. But I still had a strong sense that God was leading me and that He had a plan in place that I couldn't see yet. I was content to wait for Him to give me these things instead of trying to find them on my own.

God led me on another interesting treasure hunt that summer: He introduced me to Prissy, the little girl who still lives in my grown-up body. I learned that I needed to nurture her just as I would nurture any other child. I needed to tend to her physical and emotional needs, to discipline her in a kind and loving way, to protect her from physical and emotional harm. Like all children, she needs routines, clean surroundings, enough rest and sleep, love and affection, creative and intellectual growth, social interaction, and spiritual guidance. I realized I had been shortchanging this little girl in a number of important ways. I also realized that I had a tendency to let her have too many of her wants at the expense of her needs. God used her to show me an aspect of who I am that I would otherwise have missed. Sometimes, when things are out of kilter, I can step back and see if Prissy's needs are being met. Sometimes she's frightened and needs to have something changed in her life; sometimes she's insecure and needs reassurance from those who love her; sometimes she's tired and hungry and needs to have her physical needs met. Out of love I would do those things for my children; God showed me that that's how I should love and take care of myself, too.

As I learned to tune in to my needs, as I learned who I was — who God made me to be — I began to be free to put myself aside, and to love and care for other people. This is what God calls us to do: to care for the less fortunate; to feed the hungry; to care for orphans and widows. I finally understood what God means when He tells us to love others as we love ourselves.

This sense of freedom was new to me. Is this what Christ means when He tells us He will set us free? When we're not wearing ourselves out trying to live up to other peoples' standards, or using all our energy trying to be what other people think we should be, then we're free to live the life God wants us to live. We're free to be the person God created us to be; we're free to look to the Holy Spirit for our spiritual standard. "For freedom Christ set us free; so stand firm and do not submit again to the yoke of slavery" (Galatians 5:1). I was free! Christ had set me free from all the things and people in my life that had enslaved me, and I was finally free to look with hope on my future. Whatever that future was, I now knew who I was, and I had had my taste of freedom. I knew I was getting closer. I could hardly wait.

CHAPTER 8

Burdens Are Lifted at Calvary

HAD ONE MORE OBSTACLE TO CONFRONT. I needed to understand what had happened to us in order to be totally free from our past. I needed to be able to see that past clearly so that I didn't fall into the same unhealthy situation God had freed me from. As I was browsing through our local bookstore one rainy afternoon, my eyes landed on three books—books that almost jumped off the shelf and into my hands. As I read them I began to see how emotionally and spiritually unhealthy my past friendships and relationships had been, and how I had learned unhealthy responses to those relationships. I wanted so badly to fit in and have friends that I had unknowingly left myself behind, had become an imitation of my true self.

When I was with my Christian friends, I remember feeling as if my thoughts, my feelings, and my understandings were not important, only that I listened to and agreed with others' thoughts, feelings, and understandings. I also felt as if they were always eager to assume the worst of me instead of the best. I was never asked to explain "my side" of a situation or asked if there might be extenuating circumstances in a situation that they didn't see. It felt as if my family and I were a "project" — people to be brought in line with their interpretation of spiritual standards, instead of people on a journey just as they were. Weren't all of us people with strengths *and* weaknesses, victories *and* defeats, people who sometimes got it right and oftentimes got it wrong, people with good things from our past, and people with bad and painful things from our past? We were all on this journey of life together, but it felt as if we had been pushed to the side, that we weren't really important after all.

Jesus came to give us rest from our burdens (Matthew 11:28), and relationships based on Him should give us that same rest, not make us tired and weary. And I was *so* tired and weary! I remember wondering why when I spent time with my Christian friends I came away exhausted, when I should have come away refreshed. I always left feeling inadequate, worthless, and unappreciated, as if I had nothing worthwhile to offer. And while I couldn't quite put my finger on the problem, I found myself avoiding being around them whenever I could. I was surprised to discover, after a couple of years had passed after leaving that church, that I was actually a highly energetic and strong woman! That energy and strength had been slowly sucked out of me over the years. And while I hate to make the comparison, I felt very much like my daughter had felt when she finally left her abusive marriage. The really sad thing to me is that my old friends responded to me very much like the abusive husband: like I was the problem.

I learned that my past relationships had been based on performance: measuring up to someone else's interpretation of Biblical standards. That is a very different thing from measuring up to Christ's standard. The first standard is subject to the whims of individual people, not a moral standard set by the Church under the guidance of the Holy Spirit. Self-righteousness and judgmentalism had replaced emotional honesty and caring for human needs. Growing and thriving in that environment simply couldn't happen. It took everything I had just to survive.

Another result of spending years in that environment was that I had never learned to respect my personal boundaries. I had always been taught that having my own needs, opinions, and desires was "selfish." I thought that living the Christian life meant that I should be available to all people anytime they had a need or a desire; there was no filtering system for determining legitimate needs and discovering if I was the person who should be responding to it. As a result I had completely lost my sense of self and worth and dignity as a child of God. I felt as if God had made a mistake when He created me!

It seemed to me that the way things looked had always been more important than the reality of the way they were; that it didn't really matter that my life was a sham, so long as everyone thought I was a success. Somehow it seemed dishonest to me to be one thing on the inside and something different on the outside. God calls us to honesty and the person I was becoming was as dishonest as they come. This dishonesty was making me sick — sick in heart, sick in spirit, and sick in body.

As I began to learn and to practice the skills to find and protect my personal boundaries, as I became more sure of who I really was, as I became more honest with myself and others, as I let God show me that my life had value, I began to feel the last of the shackles fall away. I was finally in that place God had been preparing me for. I was finally ready for what He had in store for me. With no idea of what that was, I was able to say to my precious Savior, "Here I am Lord. What do you want me to do? Whatever it is, I'm Yours." Now those could be scary words. He could send me to a jungle. A desert. He could take my family from me. He could send a serious disease to live with. But I wasn't afraid. Not even a little bit! I was ready for whatever it was that He had waiting for me. I was ready to take the final steps, to go wherever He took me.

As my yearning for healthy, godly relationships grew (and to be honest, as I was ready to be a part of those relationships), I began to wonder where I'd find them. Where *were* the healthy, loving Christians? We hadn't found them (a few, to be sure, but not the majority) in any of the churches we had visited or attended over the course of our lives. Where could they be?

We were visiting our daughter's Catholic Church more and more—just to be able to go to church *somewhere* – and as I was around the people there I began to realize that these were the people I wanted to be with. Like my Catholic friend, they were kind and caring and humble; they seemed to really love each other in a quiet, steady, Christ-like way I hadn't seen before. It appeared to be the real deal, as opposed to fake friendliness and love that only looked good outwardly. More and more I knew I wanted to be part of a church family like this. I even remember thinking that I could get involved in the church activities, be friends with these people, attend Mass, but not actually *be* a Catholic. My mind settled on this as a solution to the "church dilemma." It still hadn't crossed my mind that God could be calling me to the Catholic Church, to *be* a Catholic Christian. In my mind these two words—Catholic and Christian—still did not go together, in spite of witnessing our daughter's conversion and in spite of the brief friendship I had had with Aunt Carol. I was hanging on to my belief system instead of yielding to what God had for me, and I was so blind!

But over the next many weeks, the idea of *being* a Catholic took hold in my mind, and I was in constant, earnest, pleading prayer: "Is *this* where you want me to be, Lord?" The teaching of this church seemed so contrary to everything I had been taught was truth, but I began to yearn for it in a way I didn't understand. That yearning took over every thought, every breath, every prayer. The more I asked God what *He* wanted, the more sure I was that this was what He had been calling me to. I remember also praying (a lot): "Lord, if this *isn't* what you want me to do, show me! *Please show me!*" The more I prayed that prayer the more certain I was that this was where God was leading me. After all the uncertainty, the pain, the loss, the confusion, the despair, I knew He was calling me home to His Catholic Church!

Later, when I read other peoples' conversion stories, I was always struck by the letdown I felt when they finally gave in to God's calling. One minute they were struggling and the next they submitted their will to God's will for them. Where was the drama? Where was the big event that changed their minds? But the beauty is that God doesn't work in drama and big events; He gently nudges and invites us, and the moment of yielding is soft and quiet and tender. It is a moment etched in my mind and on my soul for all eternity.

CHAPTER 9

'Tis So Sweet to Trust in Jesus

HOW WAS I GOING TO TELL MY HUSBAND that I needed to be Catholic? My journey thus far had been only my own. We never talked about what was next for us spiritually, how we might go about finding a new church home. So I didn't have any idea what his reaction would be to this announcement. I didn't know if he would divorce me. I didn't know if there would always be a strained division between us. I didn't know if we would end up living completely separate lives. I wondered about all these possibilities, but they didn't change anything. I knew with a certainty I had never known before that God had called me to the Catholic Church. Whatever my husband's reaction, I knew I would be Catholic no matter what!

We were sharing fajitas in our favorite little spot near campus when I finally worked up enough courage to tell him. I could not, in my wildest imagination, have foreseen his reaction: "I've been waiting for you." He had known for several months that *he* wanted to become Catholic, but he knew me well enough to let me finish my journey at my own pace. I can only imagine his relief that I had finally reached that point.

As we shared the things we had learned, as we talked about everything we would be giving up and leaving behind, as we talked about what our future might look like as Catholics, and as we talked about the reactions we would most likely get from some of our family, an unfamiliar peace settled over us like a warm, comforting blanket. It strengthened us and reassured us. God had been working in both our hearts in very different ways, but we had the same destination: the Catholic Church. That affirmed for us that God had surely led us to this place and that we had not arrived there by our own efforts.

So the following Monday morning, I went to the church office to sign up for RCIA. A wonderful woman there whom I had known briefly several years earlier said that she would be my sponsor. I didn't really know what that meant, but I was thrilled that someone thought it was an honor to do that for me. She would be at my side during the months-long preparation for entering the Catholic Church. She answered my questions, listened to my struggles. Here was the new friend I had been waiting so long for! I left the church office that day with more excitement, more hope, more joy than I had ever known, ever in my whole life! There really aren't words to describe the feeling of rightness that I experienced that day. And the tremendous peace kept pouring in.

That first Sunday when we knew we would become part of this amazing Church, we went to our first Mass together as potential Catholics. Our daughter explained to us how dipping our fingers in the holy water was a reenactment and a reminder of our own baptism—a physical action to help us remember a spiritual truth. She explained that we knelt before getting in our pew as a sign of reverence and acknowledgement of Christ as our King, Who is present in the tabernacle. Here was another physical action to help us remember that God is God and that we belong to Him. When we went into the church that Sunday, I remember asking God to tell me if I was doing anything that offended Him. These physical actions were so new to me, and I associated them with all the negative teachings I had been taught about the Catholic Church. So that first time I approached them cautiously and with much prayer. I couldn't see how He would have called me to this Church and then been offended by anything that was done there, but I needed to ask just to make sure.

As I entered the vestibule and timidly dipped my fingers in the holy water and made the sign of the Cross, there was no way I could have been prepared for the powerful emotion that overcame me from that simple physical action. Then as I knelt before taking my place in the pew and bowed before the Presence of my Lord, my entire being was transported straight to heaven. I could finally understand how humbling, and at the same time how powerful, it is to unite myself with Christ and His Church by these simple actions when doing them with sincere trust and whole-hearted love for Him. Once I truly understood what I was doing (not symbolizing, but *doing*), there is no way it could ever become just a ritual with no meaning. When I do them consciously and reverently, God does His part to help me focus on Him and His greatness, His holiness, His glory. As we entered our pew and knelt to pray, I felt as if I had been transported to the foot of the throne in heaven, worshiping with the angels and saints. I couldn't have left that church if I had wanted to and tried!

One of the songs the congregation sang that morning was "Amazing Grace." The words to the third verse had me choking with so much emotion I could hardly breathe. "Thru many dangers, toils, and snares, I have already come; 'Tis grace hath bro't me safe thus far, And grace will lead me home." I remember looking at my husband and seeing him choked with tears. God had brought us through so many dangers—we could have given up, or been led astray by false doctrine or empty promises—safely to our home with Him. I honestly don't know how we made it through the rest of the Mass that day. God's grace, God's mercy, God's great love had been and always would be the rudder of our lives, steering us safely through the storms and the calm times. We knew we could always count on Him because He had shown us He'd always been leading us and protecting us.

My journey so far had been strictly between my heart and my Lord. There had been no intellectual study of the Bible or of different denominations — just the Lord leading my heart and my heart following. No people were helping me decide what God was teaching me — just the Holy Spirit. And although God certainly can and does use people and books to help us learn what He wants us to know, sometimes He wants us to put them all aside and ask *Him* what He wants us to learn. He wants us to experience firsthand His holiness, His glory, His righteousness, His mercy, His great love for us. He wants us to be wholly His to do with as He wishes.

CHAPTER 10

Teach Me Thy Way, O Lord

I WAS GOING TO BE A CATHOLIC CHRISTIAN, but I had no idea what the Church actually teaches; I figured this was a good time to start learning! After a disastrous false start at our local Christian bookstore, I found myself once again at the secular bookstore. I discovered they had a pretty decent section of religious books, and more of them than I ever would have thought were Catholic. So I was in the right place (I hoped), but how would I discover which one of those thousands of books was the one I needed right then? As my eyes were skimming the titles, they zoomed in and landed on a book I knew had been written just for me: *Born Fundamentalist, Born Again Catholic*, by David B. Currie. The title seemed to say it all! I was surprised to discover that we were not the first Protestants to become Catholic, and this author sounded as if he were coming from a background similar to ours. The author's words reflected so many of my own thoughts and feelings:

hunger for God Himself, hunger for Truth, the sense of being home, the fulfillment of the deepest longings of my heart, and the surprise at finding these things where I had least expected to find them. Once I started reading, I couldn't stop. I read it straight through just to absorb the main ideas. As with any book full of meat (this one was probably milk, but for me it felt like the first real food I'd had), it took me several readings to understand it. I checked and double-checked every reference to Scripture and found myself exclaiming over and over, "I never saw that in my Bible before!"

The first—and most important—issue that I found I needed to work through was the Real Presence of Christ in the Eucharist. It was such a foreign idea to me, but as I read John 6:51-58 and 1 Corinthians 11:23-29, I began to feel as if I had been lied to my entire life! How much clearer could the Bible be? Jesus says the bread He gives for life is His flesh. He goes on to say, "Unless you eat the flesh of the Son of Man and drink His blood, you do not have life within you" (John 6:53). And "Whoever eats My flesh and drinks My blood remains in me, and I in Him" (John 6:56). No matter how hard I tried to make that sound symbolic, it just didn't. Verse 66 tells us that many disciples did not follow Him anymore. Would they have left if Jesus were talking symbolically? Wouldn't He have reassured them if that had been His intention? I was convinced that it said what it meant and it meant what it said. I was beginning to understand what the Presence had been that had drawn me into the church—it was Christ Himself in the Blessed Sacrament! The realization that I could have the reality of Christ in His presence and soon in the Eucharist (Holy Communion) completely stunned me. Christ had provided a way to be with me physically, not just spiritually, and I was just now discovering it. No wonder the people in this Church were so reverent! No wonder they were so humble! They understood that they were in the very presence of our Savior.

I had always been taught that Catholics re-crucified Christ at every Mass, and here it seemed they might be right. But Hebrews 10:10 tells us that Christ died "once for all" and that that work is complete. I began to understand it this way: Christ's crucifixion took place in A.D. 33 and it is finished; it never needs to take place again. But the benefits of that work are applied to each of us in our own time as we remember, as we take part in that event. I was beginning to understand that time is a human constraint and that God functions outside of time; the same event could be taking place two thousand years ago *and* today at the same time and be completely within God's capability. God is God, and He can do anything.

The idea that the Church is the final authority on Christian living was completely new to me. I had always been taught that the Bible—not the

Church—was our authority for faith and morals. But the author of this book challenged me to find where Scripture taught its own authority. I tried and tried, but if it's in there I—or anyone else who's tried—couldn't find it. Once again, I felt as though I had been lied to; I had been taught something that simply wasn't in Scripture.

I was beginning to understand that Christ would not have called me to a Church that didn't teach the truth. The fact that that truth didn't square with everything I had been taught my whole life was more a reflection on where I had come from than on the Catholic Church.

The next issue I needed to tackle was that of salvation. I had always been taught that if we say a prayer repenting of our sins and inviting Jesus into our hearts, then we are saved for all eternity. Done deal. Doesn't matter how we live. (At least that was the implication.) But the Catholic Church explains it this way: We are saved at a moment in time—the moment of baptism (1 Peter 3:21), but sanctification is a process that continues throughout the span of our lifetime. God molds us and sanctifies us to the extent that we let Him. So while God does the saving, we must cooperate with the process of sanctification if we're going to become what He wants us to be. And while Catholics don't believe they are saved by works, they know that works are an important part of our sanctification; they help to build our faith and they glorify our heavenly Father. It is in loving our neighbor, loving and helping the poor and needy—external works—in addition to (or rather, as a natural result of) our internal faith that we become what Christ wants us to become. And all of this is only possible by God's grace.

As I studied and learned about all the issues I needed to understand about Catholicism, I began to see an interesting pattern. No matter what my question was there was always an explanation that made perfect sense, and that explanation always came straight out of Scripture. *All* of Scripture was unfolding before my eyes in a new and wonderful way and finally making complete sense. There was no more jumping through hoops trying to make a passage or a verse make sense; no more "we can't understand what this means." Finally. Answers. Answers that don't contradict themselves. Answers that weren't someone's interpretation or opinion. Answers that haven't changed in over two thousand years. Answers that flooded my soul with peace—peace that only God can give.

CHAPTER 11

Near to the Heart of God

I WISH I COULD REMEMBER THE PRAYER. I only remember my reaction to it. This prayer was like none I had ever heard. It came from a place deep in the soul of this priest, from a heart that was on intimate terms with his Savior, from a life that is lived only to serve our Lord and His people. I remember hearing his voice wobble with emotion as he told us that we "can't out-give God." I remember thinking that if this was what it was to be Catholic I would willingly give up everything to be what the Lord wanted me to be, to be what the Lord would make me. We all have moments in our lives we can look back on and say "everything changed." And for me, everything changed in the breath of that one brief prayer.

This prayer was my introduction into the RCIA classes, where we would learn what it means to be Catholic. We would learn what the Church teaches (from the source), share our journeys with other travelers, ask our many questions, bond with people from varied backgrounds, pass through the different Rites of the RCIA process, and finally Baptism for some and Confirmation for all of us. Like all roads this one had its share of bumps and potholes, twists and turns, thrills and boredom. But in the end we were Catholics, and that's all that mattered.

We read a lot during those months. We read the Catechism (the official teaching of the Church); we read books about Church history, the Church Fathers, the saints, apologetics, doctrine, and peoples' conversions. We checked and double-checked everything we read with Scripture. I think I liked the conversion stories best, simply because they were deeply personal stories written by people who had been on journeys similar to mine. I could see God's hand at work in their lives, much as It had been in mine. People who, at the end of their particular journeys, had found peace and blessings from God they had never expected to find in the Catholic Church. They often used phrases that had become familiar to me: "I'm finally home." "I've never experienced so much peace." "My relationship with God is much more intimate." "Every longing of my heart has been fulfilled." Even though I'll probably never meet most of these people, I know them well. We have shared a journey, we have let go of the unimportant, we have faced opposition, and we are one in Christ's Body — the Church.

My husband and I started watching EWTN (Eternal Word Television Network). "Journey Home" was at the top of the list for me. Here people shared the journeys that had led them into the Catholic Church. I learned a lot from hearing their stories, and not just about the Church. I learned that there are people from many different denominations who fervently love the Lord, people who live their lives to serve Him and to love Him, people who will follow Him wherever He leads them. We have a great God Who is willing to take us just the way we are and where we are. He then molds us and helps us to mature to the degree we are willing to let Him. He can work through us wherever we have chosen to worship Him and to whatever extent we are willing to let Him work. Hearing so many stories gave me a much larger picture of God's working in humanity, of God's world, and of the diversity of God's people.

We came to know other people on this channel: humble, soft-spoken priests who drew us in with the simplicity of their preaching, lay people who shared the power of God in their lives, people whose love for the Lord influenced their whole lives. I never knew there were Catholics like that. God used all of them to show me true Catholicism, true Christianity. Little by little all these things soaked in and became part of who I am today. I don't feel altogether Catholic yet (after all, I have a lifetime of knowledge to relearn), but slowly, as I become what God wants me to be, I am becoming completely Catholic.

CHAPTER 12

Search Me, O God

*T*HIS WAS THE DAY I HAD BEEN DREADING. I had spent weeks examining my conscience and listing every sin I had ever committed. Now it was my turn to enter the confessional for the first time and to reveal all these sins before the priest I had come to have such great respect for. This "face-to-face" confession was the hardest thing I have ever done. All my faults and sins were laid bare; I was embarrassed and ashamed. Without a doubt it was the most humbling experience of my entire life. But isn't that what God asks of us — complete humility?

I would guess that most non-Catholics think, "But only God can forgive sins; a mere man can't do that." And that is absolutely correct! (Although I might argue the "mere man" point with you.) But God uses the priest's hands and voice so that we can physically hear Him say to us, "I absolve you of your sins." No words are available to me to describe that experience. Dark little places in my heart that I hadn't even realized I had been trying to hide were confessed and forgiven. That wonderful reconciliation brought tremendous joy and perfect peace. I could have sat there and basked in that contentment for the rest of my life, but I had to walk out of the confessional, do my penance (prayer and Scripture), and live my life. Still, I get to experience that fresh start, that reconciliation with the Savior, every time I go to confession.

I had a friend tell me during this time that "confession isn't Biblical." I hope she merely thought that *this form* of confession isn't Biblical, not that all confession isn't Biblical! Without a true understanding of what is really happening in the confessional, I can see how a person might come to that conclusion, but as I had learned, things are often not what we understand them to be. Jesus breathed on His disciples and said to them, "Receive the Holy Spirit. Whose sins you forgive are forgiven them; and whose sins you retain are retained" (John 20:23). So Christ Himself delegated this authority to His disciples and their successors. He knew we needed to speak our sins out loud and to actually hear His words of forgiveness, so He formulated a way to meet our need through His priestly servants. As always, God knows exactly what we need (after all, He created that need in us) and then provides a way to meet that need.

A wonderfully unexpected result of going to confession regularly is that I find myself living my life with more awareness of what I do, what I think, and what I say. I try to watch for circumstances that might cause me to sin and tread through them consciously and carefully. Of course, I do still sin—I am human—but many times I have avoided deeds or thoughts or words that would have resulted in sin.

There was one person in my life for whom I harbored truly bad feelings. These feelings caused me to go to confession repeatedly the first few months I was Catholic. I found myself asking God if He couldn't just remove this person from my life—or preferably from this earth! I had lived with those thoughts and feelings for a long time, so learning to pray for and love this person was a huge undertaking for me.

Every time I went to confession (the Sacrament of Reconciliation) and confessed these sins, my penance was to pray for him, for God to work in his life. As I prayed for him, an amazing thing happened, but it wasn't in him. It was in me. Nothing has really changed with him (at least that I can see). But now I see him as a human being, created in the image of God, worthy of dignity and respect, in need of God's saving grace. I came to understand that we're all on this journey called life and it's not for us to judge anyone else. We don't know the path God has planned for that person or where he is on his journey. After all, some of God's most effective spokesmen have come from the filthiest gutters of life. It's only for us to ask God to work in a person's heart and then stay out of His way and let Him. I've also learned to trust God with all the circumstances of this life. When this person—or anyone else—continues to hurt people and cause pain and hardship to others, I can trust that God is in control and is using all of that to accomplish His work, to bring people to Himself.

First John 1:3-4 tells us that "Our fellowship is with the Father, and with His Son Jesus Christ. We are writing this so that our joy may be complete." When my sins are confessed and forgiven, I can have fellowship with my heavenly Father, and life is full of joy I've never known before. "If we say, 'We have fellowship with him' while we continue to walk in darkness, we lie and do not act in truth. But if we walk in the light as he is in the light, then we have fellowship with one another, and the blood of his Son Jesus cleanses us from all sin" (1 John 1:6-7). I've learned that when I don't actively look for and root out the sin in my life, I'm walking in darkness—I'm living a lie. But when I look carefully at the moments of my days and acknowledge my sins before God and before His priest, I am forgiven. Fellowship is restored with my fellow man and with God and I am being completely truthful.

As a Protestant Christian I tried to confess my sins; I really did. But sometimes I just did it in passing and without any real repentance. When it's something we do in the silence of our hearts and minds, it can be easy to gloss over things we know we've done that are wrong or not done that we know we should have done. It's easy to convince ourselves that "it wasn't such a big deal," that maybe God didn't notice. But as a Catholic Christian, I try to spend a few minutes every day examining my words, my thoughts, my deeds, my omissions. Did I act like a child of my heavenly Father? Was everything I did out of love for Him? Was I critical of other people? Did I forgive those who hurt me? Did my thoughts wander in places they shouldn't? Did I take loving care of the precious earthly family God has given me? Then the last thing I do before falling asleep at night is to ask for God's unfailing forgiveness for my sins and ask for His help to overcome them. I pray a short prayer of repentance, accept His love and forgiveness, and sleep the perfect sleep of reconciliation with my Savior.

CHAPTER 13

Heaven Came Down and Glory Filled My Soul

E WERE AT THE POINT OF NO RETURN. I remember spending much of our Confirmation day in prayer—again pleading with my Savior to tell me if I was doing the wrong thing by entering the Catholic Church. All the old beliefs and voices starting swirling through my mind and I wondered if they might be right after all. But I knew that God would never let me do anything that was contrary to His will when I was begging Him to help me know that will. He would never allow me, His child, to walk into danger when I was trusting Him with everything. The more I prayed, the more He filled my being with peace and joy. Those three weeks between that first confession and my impending Confirmation had seemed an eternity, but I think the reality was that I had been waiting for this day my entire life.

When the service began that night, we knew without any doubt that we were exactly where God wanted us to be and doing exactly what He wanted us to do. Some might say that you can never be completely certain of God's will, but when you give God everything you have, listen to His voice with a clean heart (the Sacrament of Reconciliation) and complete surrender to His will, and ask to know that will with total trust, you *can* know His will—guaranteed.

Many of the details of that service—the Easter Vigil 2007—escape me. What I *do* remember clearly is the wonder of God's immeasurable love and compassion toward me as we listened to the entire sweep of salvation history from the Holy Scriptures; the awe that I felt as I heard the Gospel reading of Christ's Resurrection from the dead; the sense of community as hundreds of people responded together to the renewal of their baptismal promises; and the overwhelming love for my Savior as I—at long last—partook of His Body and His Blood in Holy Communion. Surely I glowed with the joy and happiness I was feeling. With the Psalmist I could say, "The Lord is the portion of my inheritance and my cup" (16:5), and "my cup overflows" (23:5).

There was such reverence in that church that night; the Holy Spirit was a tangible presence among us. I cried lots of tears: tears of joy, of relief, of gladness. But mostly I felt such deep gratitude to my Savior; I finally understood His great love for me.

In many ways, a very large part of my life came to an end that cold night, and the "new me" was born. My link to Protestant Christianity was severed forever, as well as to a number of friends (their doing, not mine). My new life as a Catholic Christian was born that night, a life that grows deeper every day with my Savior, a life full of amazing friends, a life of meaning and dignity and boundless joy. A life marked by deep, deep peace.

I know that life is not, nor will it ever be, easy. Christ asks us to give Him everything. He wants us to trust Him completely. He wants us to die to ourselves and to let Him live through us. He uses hard circumstances to teach us what we need to learn. He asks us to suffer with Him. But the more of ourselves we willingly give up, the more abundantly He blesses us, and He knows how to bless us beyond our wildest imagination.

Since my Confirmation my life has been marked by a settledness, a sureness that I had never known before. I feel the power of the presence of the Holy Spirit in my days; I've been marked with the stamp of God's all-consuming love. My prayer is that that power, that love will pour out of me into every person I touch as I live this life God has given me, that He will use me to make a difference in this world. My life has certain purpose as I live my days—no more coasting along or floundering. I am strong; I can do anything God asks of me because I have His constant nourishment and protection. And while it's difficult to put into words the effect my Confirmation has had on me, I trust that what words can't explain, my life somehow will.

CHAPTER 14

I Surrender All

*I*T WAS TIME FOR MY FIRST LESSON in basic Catholic living: "Offer it up." I woke up early on Easter morning—just hours after my Confirmation—to find a passionate, anti-Catholic e-mail from a long-time friend. She couldn't understand how we could have been "sucked in" by the Catholic Church, why we wouldn't find a "Bible-believing" church to be a part of. There was a long list of the errors of the Catholic Church—salvation by works, worshiping Mary, praying to statues, not following the Bible... the list went on. If the Church actually taught those things then everything she said would be true, and I would be in a cult, not God's Church!

Even though this e-mail didn't change anything I had come to learn and love about my new home, it *did* upset me that she would write such things without asking what the Church actually teaches about them. I asked our priest how I should respond to this letter, and I would like to quote part of his reply: "So, her points are valid, but she's not talking about the actual Catholic Church. She's talking about a Catholic Church that others have misinformed her about. This reminds me of one of my favorite quotations by Archbishop Fulton Sheen. He said: 'There are not one hundred people in the Unites States who hate the Catholic Church. But there are millions who hate what they *think* is the Catholic Church.' Would this be true of your friend, and perhaps many others?" And my reply was: "Absolutely!"

But what was I to do with all these hurtful things? I had tried to forgive her. I knew that trying to convince her that she didn't have the facts would be a wasted effort. The hurt and physical pain was like a tangible *thing* that had to be put somewhere, but where? I learned to give it to God – to "offer it up." Saint Paul says in his letter to the Colossians (1:24), "Now I rejoice in my sufferings for your sake, and in my flesh I am filling up what is lacking in the afflictions of Christ on behalf of his body, which is the Church." "That which is lacking in Christ's afflictions"? How can that be? How can anything be lacking? Didn't Christ do it all for us? I can't possibly understand what this means! But what I learned is that, somehow, when we "offer it up," when we give the pain to God, He uses that to build up His Church. I can't understand it, but I can see the effects of it in the people around me.

This helps me see that suffering is actually a *good* thing. It's not that we're being punished for something; it's not to be unexpected. Suffering is a sign that God is at work in our lives, molding us into godly men and women, refining the rough edges, and making us beautiful, brightly shining lights in this world. I've learned that when I grumble and complain and question God when things aren't going well, I am not happy. I'm miserable. And there is nothing there for God to use. But when I "rejoice in my suffering," when I can trust God completely with whatever "it" is, I am content. I can even be happy and joyful in spite of my circumstances, and somehow, in spite of me, God uses that. We know that whenever we get out of His way and let Him do the work, powerful and life-changing things take place around us. What a privilege it is to be used by God! The suffering, the joy, the contentment, the trust form an ever-widening circle that touches people around us in ways we will know only when we're all sharing the banquet table with our Savior in heaven.

There was an unexpected result of offering God my pain and heartache over these friends who tried to rescue me from His Church. (Unfortunately, this particular e-mail wasn't the only anti-Catholic warning I received!) When I gave the pain to God, I found that they had no more power to hurt me. I was completely free—free to live my life for my

Lord, free to love people around me, free to be more of what God wants me to be. And what else could I *ever* want to be?

CHAPTER 15

My Life Is Thine

*O*H...THE VIRGIN MOTHER OF OUR LORD... another tough issue I needed to make peace with! Catholic teaching is very clear: worship is for God alone. With that firmly in my mind, I decided that I could put her on the back burner, so to speak, and deal with her later, after I had sorted out what seemed to me to be the more urgent issues. I read several books explaining Mary's role in the Church, and while they made complete sense to me while I was reading, I didn't seem to be able to integrate any of it into my daily life.

My acceptance of and love for the Virgin Mary has been a gradual thing. I'm not sure when it happened, but I remember at some point thinking that the Church had not steered me wrong on any issue and Her teaching has never wavered, so I could trust Her with this one; I could believe it without completely understanding it. Mind you, I would never have done that with the major salvation issues, but the Church had earned my complete trust with those, so I knew I could trust Her here also.

I remember hearing in a homily that Mary *always* takes us to Jesus. That's her role. At the wedding feast in Cana (John 2:1-10), when the wine ran out, Mary noticed their problem and she took it to Jesus. She is also our role model in obedience (Luke 1:38); whatever He asks of us, our response should always be, "Whatever you want me to do, I will do willingly." When I started seeing Mary as someone other than a womb that God had used and then tossed aside, (that seems so callous to me now!) I saw that God had a place for her in the whole scheme of salvation and the Church. Her obedience gave us Jesus! What a responsibility and what a privilege to shelter the Son of God in her body, to bring Him forth, to nurse and nurture Him as a child. What agony and suffering she must have felt as she watched Him make His way to the Cross for us.

And it was suffering that began my relationship with Mary. Our family had a crisis with one of our children a few months after I became a Catholic, and once again, I found myself in our priest's office asking for help in learning how to deal with the situation. I really can't describe how scared I was for the people involved in the crisis, and how hopeless things looked to me. But after discussing everything, the priest said (and I loosely quote), "Let's ask Mary to pray with us. After all, she is a mother who has watched her Child suffer on the Cross, and she understands your suffering." As we prayed, and as Mary joined her prayer to ours, a deep peace settled over me. God was in control, and while I couldn't see the outcome, He could. I knew I could trust Him completely. Ultimately, however it turned out, He would use it for everyone's best. I had a new conviction, a new strength in that peace. I could say with confidence, "It's going to be okay. We can trust God with this situation and with our family."

Mary is becoming my firm and fast friend. I can take the deepest fears and needs and desires of my heart and ask her to pray with me about them, just as I ask my friends here on earth to pray with me. I'm gradually coming to appreciate Mary and her unique position in history, in the Church, and in my life. And while I'll never worship her — worship is for God alone — I can love her and honor her as Christ's mother, as the mother of the Church, and as my spiritual mother.

God did not drop us onto the earth two thousand years after bringing His Son into the world as flesh to figure things out on our own. We have examples throughout history to guide us in loving God the way He rightfully deserves to be loved. And that love has to reach beyond our minds to every facet of our being. We must love Him with our bodies, actions, thoughts, words, and intentions; we must be willing to give ourselves totally to Him to use in whatever way He wants. And Mary is my role model. Whatever she thought would be her life, would make her happy, she wholeheartedly gave up in order to do and to be what God had planned for her to do and to be. She had total trust in God's plan, both for herself personally and for the entire world, and she yielded herself to it with full abandon. It's easy for me to love someone I so want to be like!

CHAPTER 16

Make Me a Blessing

URING THE SPRING AND EARLY SUMMER after our Confirmation, I was acutely aware of God brushing aside pieces of my life to make room for something. But what? I had learned my lesson well: I would wait patiently for God to give it to me in His time; I wouldn't go looking for it. "It" came in the form of a phone call in mid-summer, asking if I would consider becoming our parish's food pantry coordinator. I listened carefully as the priest explained what would be required of me in that position. I tried to remain calm as I told him that I would pray about it and ask my husband what he thought. But my heart was racing and I wanted to jump up and down and shout, "*Yes!*" I *knew* this was what God had been preparing me for.

My husband had just walked in the door from a long car trip, where he had had many hours to think and to pray. (He, too, was asking God, "Now that I'm Catholic, what's next? What do you want me to be? To do? To learn?") He said he felt very strongly on that trip that we needed to become active in serving in the food pantry, both with our time and with our financial resources. When I asked God if this was what He wanted me to do, the clear answer was "*Yes!*"

So I began the process of learning the many aspects of running the ministry: keeping enough food on the shelves to feed the people who come to us for help; calling companies to ask for donations; picking up those donations; keeping track of the volunteers; actually bagging groceries and delivering them to the families waiting just outside our door; keeping track of a fair amount of paperwork; sending out reports at the end of each month and year; and keeping the pantry and appliances clean. I found that each aspect of that work was (and still is) both challenging and extremely gratifying.

One very bad habit of mine is grabbing a deal when it presents itself, without thinking through where I'm going to put it and how I'm going to get it there. One of my volunteers met me at the food bank, where we go each week to shop for free and heavily discounted food, and found a 1,057-pound bag of rice sitting beside my pickup truck. It cost eighteen cents a pound (way too good a deal to pass up), so I told the workers to forklift it onto the truck and we'd figure out a way to get it into the pantry. Now, this bag pretty much filled the back of the truck and was a little taller than I am, so we really had a challenge cut out for us. We stood there looking at that rice, praying for help, and trying to figure out a way to get it off the truck. I quickly remembered to thank God for a beautiful, clear and *dry* day. At least we didn't have rain to contend with. I'm not quite sure how we arrived at our plan, but the food bank filled my truck with flattened boxes. Then I stopped on the way to the church for packing tape, large bags, and a shovel. We assembled the boxes, lined them with bags, then shoveled the rice into the boxes (I had sterilized the shovel). The boxes of rice eventually made it onto the shelves, where we bagged it into family-sized portions to distribute it. I am very serious about getting as much food as possible into the pantry (and out to the families) at a good cost, and I totally rely on God to help us find a way to deal with the quantities. He's never let me down!

I've had people tell me that the families who come to us for help are just out to get what they can. I usually tell these people to come spend a day at the pantry and then tell me that. Although I'm sure there are some who take advantage, I think their numbers are small. Most of the families who come to us are elderly people trying to get by on Social Security or disability payments, single moms trying to make a life for their children, families where the breadwinner has lost a job, and very large families where one parent is earning a minimum wage. As soon as someone in these situations faces a crisis—injury, illness, major repair to a car or home—they have absolutely no place to turn to for survival. While there are many agencies to help, very often that can take time. In the meantime, they can come to us to have food to put on the table immediately. I have had a number of men, with tears rolling down their faces, tell me that I "just can't know" what this means to a person in need.

Many people who come to the food pantry for help are not Catholics, probably not even Christians. Christ tells us that when we feed "the least of these" we are really feeding Christ Himself (Matthew 25:35). What an honor! The reasons for the need are not my concern. My only responsibility is to love these people in a tangible, physical way, by meeting a pressing physical need in a Christ-like, loving way. I always try to pray for each person, each family who comes through our little corner of the church. God loves each one of them in a very personal way, and I am privileged to be a vehicle for some of that love. What an honor to know that God is using me in a way that touches other people's lives, in a way that makes a small difference in this world.

While we feed people's stomachs, I trust that we are also feeding their hearts. We always try to connect our hearts to those we help. If we give them just food—without caring about *them*—then we're only doing part of what God wants us to do. We need to look past their appearance, their circumstances, their intellect, and see a human being created in the image of God. And we need to love them every bit as much as we love our Savior.

It's good to have loving feelings toward those around us, but it's even better when we put ourselves totally aside and love them as Christ loves them. At the end of a day of hard, physical and emotional labor, we're exhausted, but we know we've made a small difference in our world. Hopefully, the light of Christ's love is shining a little brighter than if we hadn't worked that day. Hopefully, we've made a difference. And, hopefully, those we served saw Jesus in us today.

CHAPTER 17

Trust and Obey

I CANNOT TRUST GOD AND HAVE any fear in my heart at the same time; it's one or the other. Fear is telling God that I don't trust Him with "this issue"—whatever it is. Fear is looking on the circumstances of my life instead of keeping my gaze fixed on Jesus. Fear is forgetting that the One who created me, the One who loves me is in complete control; He knows what He is doing. And whatever He does is for my best.

I had been reading through the Old Testament, and as I was reading in the books of Exodus, Leviticus, and Numbers, God seemed to be saying to me, "Go forth fearlessly!" I began to see that when I give in to my fears and hesitate, I've given the enemy— Satan—a foothold in my heart. Whenever I take my eyes off Jesus, I let Satan have a piece of my heart, and I'm very certain I don't want him owning a piece of my personal real estate. Why would I *ever* give up God's peace, God's joy, God's love, and replace them with Satan's cheap imitations? And yet that's what I do (knowingly or not) every time I give in to fear.

"Have no anxiety at all, but in everything, by prayer and petition, with thanksgiving, make your requests known to God. Then the peace of God that surpasses all understanding will guard your hearts and minds in Christ Jesus" (Philippians 4:6-7). "Have no anxiety at all." That's a tough one!

When I think about holding a precious newborn baby, I begin to get a picture of the kind of trust God asks of us. Does the baby worry about his next meal, or wonder if anyone is going to be around the next day to care for him? No! He only knows his very real and immediate need for food or warmth or love and cries out to have that need met. And that's the infant-like trust God wants us to have in our heavenly Father. When we have a need—physical, emotional, spiritual—He wants us to cry out for Him, so that *He* can fill that need and care for us. We need never worry or fear for tomorrow, for our great God is our loving Father and always gives us exactly what we need.

"But in everything, by prayer and petitions, with thanksgiving make your requests known to God." God already knows what we need, but we need to ask, we need to come to our Father. That's what He wants from us—for us to recognize that we need Him. I've heard many times that the thankfulness is for knowing that God will take care of our needs. But I wonder if perhaps the thanksgiving is simply expressing our gratefulness that we have such a loving Father who cares so much for us, that we can approach Him, even with our human frailties and our simple, childlike trust. And there is simply no room for fear in that trust.

"*Then* the peace of God that surpasses all understanding will guard your hearts and minds in Christ Jesus." Wow! After we've trusted Him completely, after we've taken our needs to Him, *then* He gives us peace. (Wouldn't it be easier if He gave us the peace first, *then* asked us not to have anxiety?) But He's given us the freedom to reject or choose that peace by our actions. And when we choose that peace, it guards our hearts and minds in Christ Jesus. Could it be that our hearts and minds are guarded from Satan? Could it be that when our hearts, our lives are overflowing with that peace, then there is simply no room for anything but our Savior? There is no room for fear?

Move forward fearlessly. Trust God completely. Let Him work in me. "Do not fear or be dismayed, for the Lord, your God, is with you wherever you go" (Joshua 1:9).

I was recently on a prayer retreat, and in the desk I found this poem:

God asks us
To move in faith,
In darkness,
In unknowing —
But move we must.
    (Father Tom Zoeller)

That's complete trust; that's fearless trust in our great God.

"Blessed may you be, O Lord, God of Israel our father, from eternity to eternity. Yours, O Lord, are grandeur and power, majesty, splendor, and glory. For all in heaven and on earth is yours; yours, O Lord, is the sovereignty; you are exalted as head over all. Riches and honor are from you, and you have dominion over all. In your hands are power and might; it is yours to give grandeur and strength to all. Therefore, our God, we give you thanks and we praise the majesty of your name" (1 Chronicles 29:10-13).

This is my God. I will choose to trust Him.

CHAPTER 18

O Worship the King

❀

*G*OD CREATED US TO BE people who celebrate. We celebrate small occasions: baby's first steps, a good report card, a raise. We celebrate big occasions: a birth, a graduation, a wedding. We anticipate these celebrations. We prepare for them. We remember them long after they've passed. But the most important celebration for a Catholic is the Mass. We anticipate it; we prepare for it. (At least we should prepare!) I can read the Scripture passages for the week; I can pray for God to open my heart to what He has to teach me; I can ask Him to open my heart in love to those around me. Sunday Mass feeds me and gives me the grace I need to live out my life. Mass is not an inconsequential hour that interrupts my week; it is the essential high point of my week!

As I enter the church, I'm thankful for two sets of double doors, a place to shift from the busyness of the world and prepare myself for God's presence, a place to quiet my mind. The first thing Catholics do when they enter the church is to dip their fingers in the holy water and make the sign of the Cross. It's a reminder that we belong to Christ. He died for us, He rose from the dead, and in our baptism, we also die to ourselves and rise up to a new life. We are physical creatures, and we need physical reminders of who we are and who Christ is.

At my pew, I kneel before my Lord and Savior, another physical reminder that Christ is my King and I am His humble servant. I can never put myself in authority over someone else, because we are all servants of the King. As soon as I am in my pew, I kneel and pray—more time to quiet my mind and spirit and to be one with my Lord. This is a time to examine my conscience and ask forgiveness for my sins, a time to bring the needs of the day before my heavenly Father, a time to simply be with Him.

A spirit of gathering prevails as the priest and altar servers process to the front of the church. We are all coming together as one body in faith; our very presence is an encouragement to everyone assembled. We are asked to reflect on God's great mercy, for it's that mercy that sustains us; what a gift to spend time pondering its meaning for me. Chills run down my spine after our general confession of sins when the priest concludes with, "May almighty God have mercy on us, forgive us our sins, and bring us to everlasting life." Those are not just words. They are petitions—hope for this week, this

life, and eternal life. The prayer summarizes everything God does and has done for us; it breathes fresh
life into my lungs every time I hear it.

We've asked God for mercy, for forgiveness, for
life. Next we sing "Gloria," a hymn of joyful praise
to God, not for what He does for us, but for Who
He is. "Glory to God...Lord God, heavenly King...
almighty God and Father...Lord Jesus Christ...Son
of the Father...Lamb of God...the Holy One...the
Most High." My heart *needs* to sing these praises to
God — we were created to sing them! My heart is full
of awe for God.

Silence is a special gift included in the Mass. At
first, I was a little uncomfortable with it because I
wasn't used to it and I wasn't sure what to do with
it. But now I know to use it to realize that I *am* in
God's presence, to tell Him how much I love Him,
and to bring Him my petitions. As the priest then
prays, all the needs of the congregation are offered
to God through Christ.

After a common "Amen," we prepare for the
Scripture reading. The first reading is usually from
the Old Testament and ties in directly to the theme
of that day's celebration. This is followed by a
responsorial Psalm, a time for us to respond to God's
Word — not just hear it. God's Word always demands
a response from us, an indication that it has touched
us, changed us. The words of the Psalmist remind
us of our great need for God — His mighty power,

His strength, His kindness, His mercy, His love. The second reading is usually from the Epistles. Again, its theme is tied to the day's theme; nothing is ever random or isolated. At the end of each reading we are reminded, this is "the Word of the Lord," and we respond, "Thanks be to God." We get to voice our acknowledgment and our thankfulness.

We sing "Alleluia" as we joyfully anticipate hearing Christ's own words read to us in the Gospels. We celebrate the reading and prepare for it. Part of the preparation for this reading is signing small crosses on our forehead, our lips, and our heart. We are reminding ourselves to keep these words in our minds, on our lips, and in our hearts — another physical act to help us live the lives God wants us to live, and that God uses to strengthen us. We stand during this reading out of respect for Christ's Word, for He and His Words are one. The congregation concludes the reading with "Praise to You, Lord Jesus Christ." Just words? Never! It's another opportunity to lift our voices in praise to the One to Whom praise belongs.

The readings are followed by the homily. Homilies are usually fairly short, to the point, and not the main event of the Mass. In them we are called to live holy lives, to be brightly shining lights in a dark world, to apply the lessons of Scripture to our lives today. I never walk away wondering what the point was or how I could apply it to my life. I feel strengthened, challenged, and blessed.

Then we stand and recite the Nicene Creed, a common confession of our faith. I am reminded that I am one part of a large body, that we are a community, a family. We don't each believe in different things; we are truly one. We belong here. We are wanted here. We come from different cultures, different economic backgrounds, and different ways of life, but here, we are one. We have the same faith, the same Lord. This is a perspective of Christ's Church I never thought about before; I *knew* it, but I never saw that it was relevant to my own life. God has opened my eyes to His universal Church; I am part of a body much larger than I ever realized. We get to cherish our diversity and our universality each week as we celebrate our Lord together. I feel that God is telling me, "I want to give you the whole world, not just one little piece of it. I want you to see the bigger picture. I want you to love *all* of these precious people as I love you." I'm awed and humbled as I receive anew this gift each week as we profess our faith together. God is a God of unity, and that can happen only as we consciously and individually unite ourselves to *all* His people. And we can do it by reciting "I believe" together.

Next, we pray for the needs of all people. I'm always overwhelmed as I consider that it's not just this Church body praying for these very needs—it's every Catholic Church in the world. I can almost see the prayer rising up to heaven from every part of the earth, a tangible force in its unity. What power! We all cry to our Father for the needs of the human race, and we all respond to each petition with "Lord, hear our prayer." I'm reminded of the man who was not even willing to lift his eyes to heaven as he cried out, "O God, be merciful to me, a sinner" (Luke 18:13). We cry out — in one voice — to God for mercy, on us and on the whole world.

We now shift our focus to our preparation for the Eucharist — thanksgiving for Christ's sacrifice on our behalf, the thanksgiving for all that we have been blessed with in this life and the life to come, thanksgiving for the opportunity to participate in that great sacrifice. We begin this part of the Mass with the priest inviting the children to bring their offerings. And — this *is* a Catholic Church — the children pour out of the pews, too numerous to count. Even the smallest children who are barely able to walk bring their pennies, their quarters, their dollars. I love to watch them walk, run, and dance up the aisles to put their treasures in the basket. The priest always greets them with a smile and delight at their presence. Even though there is always a low-level and sometimes not-so-low-level of children and babies fussing, crying, and being children, I love that they are just as important as each older child and adult present. They are part of the *all* who have gathered. They are priceless gifts from God and are treated as such; they merit as much dignity and respect as every adult. Then the baskets are passed for everyone else to give their offerings. The priest prepares for the bread and wine, and when all is ready, a family brings the gifts to the altar: the bread and wine, our monetary offerings, sometimes a collection of food for the needy, the book of intentions (prayer requests). We offer everything that we have, everything that we are, our needs, our requests; these are all joined to Christ's sacrifice on the Cross for us. We offer it all back to God to use for His glory, His praise, His Church. After a brief prayer of thanksgiving, the congregation sings "Holy, Holy, Holy Lord." We've given Him everything that we are and have, we've thanked Him for Christ's sacrifice, and now we acknowledge His holiness, His power, His glory. It's our right and joyous response to everything that He is and does.

The Eucharistic prayers give God His rightful thanks and praise; they implore the Holy Spirit to make present the Body and Blood of our risen Savior in the bread and wine. We are joined to Christ. We offer our sacrifice and Christ gives Himself to us in the Eucharist.

We stand and pray the Lord's Prayer together. The more I pray this prayer, the more deeply meaningful it becomes. "*Our Father!*" We can call the God of the universe "Father!" He gathers me close and holds me in His arms, because I'm His child and He's my Father. If it stopped there, it would still be everything. He's in heaven and His name is Holy; that puts Him in His rightful place and me in my rightful place.

Sometimes I want to be God, to have things go the way I want them to go, but I see life's circumstances only through my limited lenses. I see only the present. He is omnipotent. I can trust that He is the One Who truly knows. "Thy will be done on earth as it is in heaven." That means me — it's not a generalized statement. I need to seek His will and then do what He wants me to do.

"Give us this day our daily bread." It's not just physical food, it's spiritual food, Christ. And He gives it as we need it; we can trust that there will always be enough for tomorrow.

"Forgive us our trespasses as we forgive...." "As we forgive." That can be so hard! And yet there is such freedom in forgiveness. It takes energy to hold a grudge, to not forgive. But God tells us to do it, for our good as well as for the one who hurt us. His forgiveness is complete when we have done our part.

"Deliver us from evil." The footnote in my Bible says, "...from the Evil One." Every day, I am protected from Satan by God Himself. Talk about security! I know Satan wants to push me into the ditch, but God protects me.

"The kingdom, the power, and the glory are yours, now and forever." It's all His; He is everything. And still He loves me, with all my faults, sins, and frailties. I'm left speechless and in awe.

After the prayer, as I come back to earth, we are given the opportunity to "offer each other a sign of peace." Here is a time to share that peace with those around us; a time to be blessed by peace from those we don't see in the course of our week. We are learning that we are all Christ's body; we are all one.

My favorite part of the Mass—aside from actually partaking of the Eucharist—is saying together: "Lord, I am not worthy that You should enter under my roof, but only say the word and my soul shall be healed." God has used those words to heal wounds so deep I never thought could be healed. But layer by layer, they *have* healed, and I know it's only through God's great mercy that He speaks the word that accomplishes that. I am not worthy, but He can and does give me the gift of worthiness so that I can eat the Bread that gives me life. What a great God!

And then, humbly and reverently, we proceed to the altar to partake of that life in the Body and Blood of our Lord, Jesus Christ. As I kneel in my pew afterward, I watch hundreds of people come quietly for their turn: young people, children, parents holding babies, elderly people, crippled people, dark-skinned people, light-skinned people, well-dressed people, and poor people. We have all come for one thing: to worship—to receive the life of our Lord. Sometimes I'm so overcome with emotion I wonder if I'll ever have the strength to leave. *This* is where I want to be!

But at the end of the Mass we are called to "go forth and serve God and one another." We're called to go out into the world to share Christ with those we meet during the week; we're called to *be* Christ to the people around us. Jesus told His disciples, "Go, therefore, and make disciples of all nations..." (Mathew 28:19). "And, behold, I am with you always, until the end of the age" (Matthew 28:20). He is with us, with you, with even me. In the Eucharist, in the Holy Spirit, in the encouragement we receive from those around us, He has provided for our every need.

CHAPTER 19

Praise My Soul, the King of Heaven

OMETIMES GOD TAKES US TO A PLACE we never thought we'd be, a place we never thought we wanted to be, even a place we always thought we never wanted to be. The road to that destination can be long, hard, and lonely. I suffered many wounds on my journey, and pain and fear and grief were my constant companions. My husband and I made such a journey; we traveled in the same deep, dark valley, but we traveled different roads. God, in His great compassion and mercy, brought us to the same destination—the Catholic Church—by very different experiences and circumstances.

As long and difficult as my journey was, I wouldn't trade a single minute of it, for it was in that valley that God taught me to rest in Him. He taught me that sometimes it's okay—even good—just to "be." He taught me to hear His still, quiet voice in the midst of the loud, insistent voices all around me.

There in the valley, God taught me to see His hand at work in my life and to wait patiently for His timing.

I came home to the Catholic Church in April of 2007. Here is where I find a constant outpouring of God's goodness and mercy, God's tremendous joy and peace, God's healing and hope. I am surrounded by my new family — a family who forgives me, loves me, strengthens me, comforts me, encourages me, and teaches me. It is a place where I am free to be the person God created me to be, a place where I can live a life of service, a place where I am learning to trust my Savior completely. It's a place of healing, of hope, of dignity and respect. I am learning what it means to suffer with Christ. I have a much deeper communion with Christ, and I'm trying to learn to live a life of self-sacrifice. God has given me every desire of my heart; what more could I want?

My only response can be to praise Him and thank Him for His amazing love, His constant compassion, His unimaginable peace, His exhilarating joy, His gentle forgiveness, His quiet rest, His unending grace, His great mercy, His total healing, His sure strength, His soothing comfort; to give Him every-thing that I am and everything that I have; to trust Him with all the circumstances of my life.

My prayer is for you to have the courage to ask God to show you where He wants you to be and then to be willing to follow Him wherever He leads you — even if that is into the Catholic Church. If you do, I promise He will not disappoint you; He will bless you beyond your wildest imagination. He will heal you and strengthen you; He will give you peace beyond human understanding and joy that makes you want to dance in the streets shouting out the goodness of your Savior. He will give you new hope for the future, no matter the circumstances you find yourself in now. He will give you a new home, a new family, a new freedom to be who you were truly meant to be. I can tell you without the slightest doubt that when you give Him everything you have to give, He will give you everything He has to give. And the God of the universe truly has everything to give.

Bless the LORD, my soul;
All my being, bless his holy name!
Bless the LORD, my soul;
do not forget all the gifts of God,
Who pardons all your sins,
heals all your ills,
Delivers your life from the pit,
surrounds you with love and compassion,
Fills your days with good things;
your youth is renewed like the eagle's.
(Psalm 103:1-5)
Amen. And Amen.

PART II

Learning to Soar: Suffering

CHAPTER 20

Precious Lord Take My Hand

TWO YEARS AFTER MY CONVERSION to the Catholic Church, I was diagnosed with an aggressive form of breast cancer. For almost a year I had been aware that God was preparing me for something hard, but I had no idea what it would be, and trying to convey that knowledge in words is almost impossible, for God works in our souls in ways that are beyond our perception, comprehension, and expression.

One of the rituals of parenthood is sorting through our children's clothes and toys. Through the years I have spent countless hours sifting through the piles: this is worn out; this is too small; this is broken or missing parts; this is no longer useful. As a wise parent weeds out the old to make room for the new, so God weeds through the "stuff" of our lives to make room for the new gifts He wants to give us. We—at least I—often try to fill the void this leaves with our own "stuff" —friends, activities, work — instead of waiting for God to give us *His* gifts. He wants to give us the best, and the very best gift is God Himself. As my surgeon removed the tumors from my body, so God removed the "tumors" from my soul: the self-centeredness, the impatience, the presumption, the uncharitable attitudes, the pride, the impurities of my heart. I was left feeling physically and spiritually impoverished. Thankfully I was too sick to try to fill the void their removal created; I could only wait for God to do it for me. And He filled that void so wonderfully with Himself that I cannot regret the year of suffering that I endured.

I find it important to share an experience I had about six months before I discovered the tumor under my arm. I was trying to take a nap on the sofa one afternoon, and somewhere between wakefulness and sleep I had a dream. A vision. I don't know what it was, but it was very real. High above the earth I was soaring with the eagles. I felt the cool wind on my face, the warm sun on my back. Joy. Peace. Freedom. Quiet. It was like playing in the waves in the ocean, but it was the air that carried me instead of the water. What happened next brought me out of the dream/vision. I heard the voice of God say: "I want to teach you how to soar with the eagles." If someone else had told me this had happened to her, I might have been skeptical, but it happened to me, and it was as real as the air I breathe.

So on Easter Sunday morning when I felt a ping-pong ball-sized lump under my arm, I knew that it was time for me to learn how to soar. I didn't know where that journey would take me, but I knew that my heavenly Father held me safe in His arms. My emotions and my imagination began a roller-coaster ride as I wondered which turn my life was about to take. One train of thought took me down the "if it's cancer" road. What kind of treatments would I accept or reject? How could I tell my family? Would I survive it or was this the beginning of my journey home to my Savior? Then I went down the "chances are good that it's not cancer" road. That line of thinking caused me to consider my days. Was I spending enough time with the people I love? Was I doing what was really important? Were there things I wanted to do while I was still on this earth?

My husband and I each seemed to be locked in our own world of silence, trying to prepare ourselves for whatever might be coming. Sometimes we talked, but without knowing what we were facing there was nothing concrete to talk about; so we wondered and prayed in silence. But the good thing — the sure thing — was that God was in the silence. My mind was all over the place, trying to prepare for every eventuality, but my emotions were good and I still prayed for whatever would bring God glory.

I asked myself a thousand times if I was afraid. There was not an easy answer. Was I afraid of dying? No! I had confident hope that my eternity was secure with my Savior; the joys that await me there are beyond my imagination. I might have been afraid for my husband, my children, my grandchildren, and my mother. I know how hard it is to lose someone you love, and I felt their grief. My own words kept coming back to me: "You cannot trust God and have any fear in your heart at the same time. It's one or the other." I really did trust, but sometimes I had to fight to overcome the fear to get to the trust… And the waiting to know what we were facing was so hard! I knew that God's grace was sufficient to see me through that trial and I prayed that it would bring glory to my precious Savior. It was very freeing to be able to pray that and to mean it unreservedly. As we waited, I prayed, "Lord, help me to keep my focus on You and on others; don't let me turn in on myself. Help me live my days freely and for You. And if I need to give my family hard news about this, please prepare the way. My life is in Your hands."

It was finally the day to go for my mammogram and I wondered how the day would end. Would I know what I was facing? Would I have to wait some more for news? We discovered that day that there were *three* masses in my breast instead of the one I was expecting. It seemed like an "add-on" that I had to come to grips with, that "what I was facing" was growing bigger and bigger by the day. The technician immediately scheduled an appointment with a surgeon's first opening four days later. She said that tumors are graded by their likelihood of being cancer, and mine was a "grade 4" — almost certainly cancer. I found that I didn't have the emotional energy to share that news with our family, so my wonderful husband did that for me.

For me, one of the hardest parts of that waiting game was knowing how to respond to friends' and acquaintances' comments. I knew that they were trying to be encouraging and optimistic, but their words very often triggered frustration and tears. Hearing, "It's probably nothing," or "You shouldn't expect the worst," didn't help me to mentally prepare for what might lie ahead. "I'm sorry" often came across as sappy and I didn't handle that well at all. Sometimes even a hug felt wrong! I needed my friends to come up beside me and say, "I'm here. You're not alone." I needed them to help me have courage. I never could figure out how to explain that to them, and then I wondered why I felt like I had to explain myself anyway. It was my journey, my struggle. I needed my friends to respect that process of binding my spirit to God's spirit, where I knew I would find the strength I needed to get through whatever was coming. I simply didn't have enough energy left to help anyone else deal with it. So I snuggled in with my "safe" people: people who respected my feelings and left me free to work through my emotions without trivializing them; people who accepted my bad days and didn't make me feel like I had to pretend that I was having a good one. I had had it with the interminable waiting, the lack of sleep and appetite, the shortness of breath, the discomfort. I was at the end of my rope. Spiritually I was good, but emotionally not so much. I wondered if I could whine before I offered it all up.

We saw the surgeon and scheduled a biopsy for the following Monday. She would remove all three masses during that procedure. I knew I would be pretty sore, but without the "ping-pong ball" under my armpit, I hoped that I might be able to sleep again.

We finally said "cancer" out loud. It felt awkward at first, but we needed to be able to say it. That was the first day that I felt like I had any fight in me. I imagine sleep played a big part in that; I had taken a pain pill the night before and had slept for the first time in ages.

The weekend before my surgery was quiet. I was able to relax, smile and laugh, and that felt so good! I talked to my mom and all our kids, made peace with the waiting, and we went for surgery early on Monday morning. I was ready to have those "unfriendly guests" leave my body! The radiology department was my first stop. Two masses couldn't be located by feel, so they used the mammogram to locate them, then inserted wires into them for the surgeon to find. Not the most fun hour of my life!! I woke up after the surgery in more pain than I ever thought possible! The nurse told me that they had given me all the pain medication they could and it was time to go home. I don't think I've ever seen my husband react so fast!! He told the nurse to call the doctor, that I wasn't going anywhere in that kind of pain. The doctor did order two more doses of something that did the trick. I vaguely remember getting dressed and hoping I wouldn't throw up on the trip home. And then I was completely out.

After the surgery the doctor told Ken she thought there was a 12% chance that the two smaller lumps were cancer, and the large one she thought was a sure bet. The waiting that day seemed a little out-of-body. God reminded me that I knew how to soar. He also reminded me to take this one day—one wave—at a time.

Author's Note: At a silent retreat I had attended in January, I was given Isaiah 43:1-6 to meditate and pray on. My instructions were to pray those verses for an hour, then write whatever God gave me. I fell asleep before I could write anything, but woke up at four o'clock the next morning, and this is what I wrote:

"I had a vivid image of playing in the waves at the beach. Real waves! The sun is shining. The breeze is cool. The water is icy cold. There is such joy, such freedom in just playing in the water, just being alive. It is so exhilarating! God loves me so much that He lets me play. I can't control the waves; all I can do is go with their flow, be happy to be in the water, enjoy it the way it is. Don't try to change anything! Glorious freedom! Glorious exhilaration!

"Perspective. At the edge of this great ocean, there is perspective. God's creation is beyond my comprehension. God is beyond my comprehension. And yet He loves me; I'm precious to Him. He is always with me. And, like playing in the waves, I shouldn't try to change anything—just go with the flow, the rhythm that is already there. And enjoy it! Enjoy my precious Savior! When He says He is—and will be—with me, His power and His might give me strength for the challenges and trials of life. When I play in the waves I am totally in the moment—no thoughts about anything except the exhilaration of the play. I need to be living my life like that, too. Be in the moment, focus on the right now without fretting about what is coming next or what is not getting done.

"Like the water in the ocean, there are no limits with God. He is infinite. But I can limit God like trying to put water in a jar

and calling it the ocean. Don't be afraid to let
Him be God!! Trust Him. Enjoy Him. Glory
in His strength, His power, His freedom, His
joy, His peace. He loves me enough to give
me this small pleasure. He loves me enough
to take pleasure in my delight."

I didn't know how, but somehow this tied in
with the "move forward fearlessly" theme that God
was teaching me. The "do not fear" came up everywhere! It was important not to be overwhelmed
by all the possibilities facing me, but it was also
important to keep my eyes on those waves. I had to
be realistic about my situation, but still only take it
one thing, one day at a time.

Friday of that week might have been the most
bizarre day of my life! Our grandson was born, and
I was too sick to be there to see him. The surgeon
called to tell me the pathology report had come in
and I definitely had cancer. It was a day filled with
every emotion! Waiting anxiously for our grandson's arrival; finally knowing something, even if
it was hard; laughter at my "loopiness" and fried
brain from the pain pills; quiet as we all worked our
way through the news.

How was I dealing with that news? There was an
eerie calmness surrounding me; a sure confidence
that I was in my Savior's hands. There was also a
dread for what the next weeks and months might

bring. I felt "numb" from the drugs and the news. I still wanted to do "this" well, but had no idea how to do that! Maybe it went back to simply "being" and letting God do the work. The reality of my situation came to me gradually: there was not going to be an easy fix! My question in all of this was: "How do I keep living my life, or does this become my life?" I wished I knew.

It hurt me to see my family in pain and not be able to change those circumstances for them, and seeing the pain my husband suffered was unbearable! And yet I was helpless; it was completely out of my control. This was where the "trusting God" got hard; it was a real struggle to give it all to Him and not try to "fix it" myself. But, really, why would I want to do that, even if I could? I knew that to get in His way would just make a mess of His work; so the trick was to let go and let Him do what He was doing in that situation. I remember praying, just days after finding the lump, that I was willing to go through whatever it took for God to accomplish His purpose and to bring glory and honor to Him. It was a little easier to pray that when I didn't know what was coming, but it still continued to be my prayer. I think I got a better picture of Christ in the Garden of Gethsemane praying, "Not as I will" (Matthew 26:39). I just prayed that I could continue to say, "Not as I will," as I went through the days and weeks ahead. I prayed for the peace of God to be such a visible part of my journey that it had to make a difference to those around me.

I had a revelation that week about my illness: there were people that I couldn't talk to about my faith, but—boy—I had their attention!! I knew they would be watching closely and this might be the only "Christ" they would ever see. What a privilege! What a responsibility! But what if I failed? What if I didn't do it well? I knew that *I* couldn't do it, but I prayed that God's strength would shine through, that Christ's peace would be evident. Only He could do this for me. I realized that I might never know the work that God was doing through my illness, but He did, and I knew it was good, that He knows what He is about. So it was time for me to put actions to my words and move forward fearlessly and trust myself, my family, and my friends into His loving care.

CHAPTER 21

In My Life, Lord, Be Glorified

O N WEDNESDAY OF THE FOLLOWING WEEK, we arrived at the clinic for my MRI. After changing into my "fashion conscious" gown, they started another IV. I dreaded all those IVs; they tended to use veins in my wrist and they *hurt*! It got to be more than I could bear, but I learned to take a deep breath and "offer it up." I remember feeling as if I had entered some kind of altered universe. A universe where women roamed windowless hallways, entered windowless rooms filled with space-age looking machines. Where women were eerily silent, each deep in her own worries and experiences. Where smiles were tenuous at best. The events in the "other" universe seemed irrelevant and unimportant. It felt weird to bounce between those two universes. But I did.

The MRI was quite an experience. They positioned me face down on the machine, then gave me earplugs and headphones to dull the loud, banging noises of the machine. The pressure on my forehead gave me a headache, and it was hard to stay still in such an uncomfortable position. I decided to pray the rosary for the twenty minutes or so I was in the machine. As I prayed, I went to a place deeper within myself than I'd ever been before. At the same time that it was deep within, it felt as if I were outside my body, not exactly seeing myself, but as though my spirit were hovering. I was aware of all the noise and discomfort, but that wasn't where I was. I never could find the words to describe that experience!

When we were finished and my dizziness had passed, the technician told me to wait a few minutes while the doctor looked at the results. A short wait turned into a long wait; then they told me they needed to do another ultrasound. They found another small lump in a different part of my breast and ordered a needle biopsy. While it wasn't the worst thing I had ever experienced, I hope I never have to do it again. I was still really sore two days later. But we finally had some good news: that biopsy was negative.

When all the MRIs and scans were finally done, we met with the oncologist. We didn't know if we would have to make treatment decisions that day or if we'd have some time to think about our options. I needed time. I was tired and used up, and I couldn't seem to escape from that "numb" place I was in. I remember wondering if I could wake up and discover that it was all a bad dream! And then

I wondered where that thought came from. A few days later I resettled into that peaceful place where I remembered that God is faithful, God is merciful, and God knows what He is about. And while cancer still consumed my thoughts, for a few moments here and there, I could forget that I had cancer. I could be myself again, because, while I had cancer, that was _not_ who I was. I was still me and I would have to fight to keep myself from getting lost in that bizarre disease.

Over the weekend, I felt as if God were asking me to give Him my life. Not the activity of my days, but my very breath. I knew that it was His and He could take it whenever He wanted to, but this was different; He was asking me to voluntarily give it to Him. And I did. No questions. No reservations. No hesitation. But how was I to help my husband, my kids, my grandkids, and my mom understand? They wanted to fight to keep me with them, and I could understand that, but God had to be first! I needed to remember to pray for them. Sometimes I forgot that God had prepared me, but they weren't in that same safe place.

We finally saw the surgeon and scheduled another surgery—an axillary lymph dissection. (I think that's what she called it.) She would remove lymph nodes under my arm and then do another biopsy. She said that doing chemo and radiation would give me my best chance of survival. I asked her what my prognosis looked like and she said, "Honestly, it's up for grabs. The small size of the primary tumor with the large size of the third (lymph) tumor is aggressive and worrisome."

I needed to learn how to stay on an "even keel" when people around me were sad or full of pity for me. (I *hated* that!!!) I wanted them to catch my attitude of trust and confidence in my precious Savior. Our priest helped me learn how to not fall into the trap of being sucked into other peoples' emotions. He said that when they express those emotions, they are expressing their *opinions* about the situation. I needed to remind myself of that and keep my gaze fixed on Jesus. Others may have felt pity for me, but I knew the truth: God was using me to bring glory to His Holy Name. If I could keep my focus on that I would never get sucked in again.

I had a week when I almost felt like my old self—almost energetic. I also had some good stretches of time when I didn't think about cancer, and that felt even better! I tried not to dread my next surgery, but I did. And I <u>always</u> dreaded the days I had to take pain pills; they just made me feel weird and not at all myself. This surgery would tell us if I were battling Stage 2 or Stage 3 cancer. I knew I had a battle ahead of me and I would need my family and friends' prayers for strength and courage in a way I had never needed them before. "When you go out to war against your enemies and you see horses and chariots and an army greater than your own, do not be afraid of them, for the LORD, your God, who brought you up from the land of Egypt will be with you.... Be not weak-hearted or afraid; be neither alarmed nor frightened by them. For it is the LORD, your God, who goes with you to fight for you against your enemies and give you victory" (Deuteronomy 20:1-4).

God gave me another wave analogy. When you play in the water at the beach and you want the security of the ocean floor, you are at the mercy of the breaking waves. They knock you down, pull you under, and wear you out. But when you go out to deeper water, where you can't "touch bottom," and relax, the water holds you up and you just float over the top of the waves. But, once again, I had to do my part!! I was free to choose how far out from shore I would play. I had to go there of my own free will.

I woke up early the next morning ready to go into surgery with a positive attitude. I knew I was in my Savior's loving hands; where else would I want to be? I asked the anesthesiologist to put me under, *and then* put my arm out on the board; I didn't think I could do that voluntarily. I woke up in an unbelievable amount of pain again, but the nurse kept giving me medication until I could bear it. That time I struggled with throwing up — great fun right after surgery! And then I was totally knocked out. The days after that were a blur, but there were a couple of things that made their way to my fuzzy brain. First, the doctor said she removed nine more lymph nodes and they were all cancer-free. Somehow, having it fairly "contained" seemed less overwhelming to me. Second, I was vaguely aware of some really good friends coming for a quick visit. After they left I fell into a deep, deep (drugged) sleep and slept about fourteen hours. The next day I was a little wobbly, but I decided to try to make it until evening without taking a pain pill.

As I was lying in bed that night, I pondered the "What was a cross is now a gift" statement I had heard at a retreat a couple of years before. I heard God's voice telling me, "This is a gift." I tried to wrap my head around that. I believed it. I accepted it. I just couldn't quite figure out what it meant! I guessed that even if I couldn't understand it, I still needed to thank the Giver for the gift. So I did. I thanked the Lord for the gift of this cancer.

I spent the next week resting and taking life at a very slow pace. I wanted to get back to my "normal" life, but a little more relaxed, a little more deliberate. I had to sort out the activities of my life and let go of the less important ones. I was looking forward to a lull between surgery and treatment. Quiet times, time with family, working my way back to the food pantry, an organ lesson, a trip to Silver Dollar City theme park with my sister, lunch with friends, a few house projects. As usual, my list was longer than the time available, so I did what I could and let the rest go.

Eleven days after surgery I began to feel pretty good again. My incision was still sore and there were numb places down my arm, but I was feeling much better. I could move my arm, but still needed to keep it elevated quite a bit throughout the day. I resigned myself to chemo and radiation; since we didn't remove the breast, there may not have really been a choice. The oncologist told me that the chance of the cancer returning in the next couple of years was about 40% if I didn't do any treatment; with chemo, that chance went down to 27-28%. I wondered how to balance extending my life with the quality of that life. How did I know when to fight for that life and when to let it go? I felt pulled between two worlds.

Mass that weekend was very emotional for me. God's love and Christ's presence were all I felt. For one glorious hour I was at the foot of the throne in heaven, praising my Savior with the Church that is not defined by time or place. For one hour I could almost grasp God's amazing love for me. For one hour I could almost grasp the great mystery of our Trinitarian God. And then I was sent out into this very earthly world to live my life that week. But I wasn't sent alone. The power of the Holy Spirit was with me: to guide me, to help me, to give me strength. The power of Almighty God was with me: to love me, to pour His love through me to others, to protect me from harm. And Jesus Christ, the only begotten Son of the Father, was with me: to save me from my sins, to help me live a righteous and holy life, to give me the victory in Him. So I could do what needed to be done that week because He has promised He will never leave me nor forsake me. He is all I need.

I remembered another experience I had had during Mass a few months before. It had been one of those Sundays when my heart soared above this earthly life and met God's Sacred, all-consuming Heart. I had just returned to my pew after receiving the Body and Blood of my precious, Holy Savior, and as I knelt in my pew, I began to watch people coming to partake. Hundreds of them of every description. Old and young; sick and well; poor and rich—all here for one thing: to share in the life of our Lord. As I was watching, my heart burned with intense love for all of those people—and for each of those people. Then I understood that God was giving me as much of a glimpse as my humanity could understand of His love, of how He loves me. It was as if, for one brief moment, I shared His Heart and felt His love for all His people. Somehow, I think God was using that experience to burn His love into my heart and life. How could I explain such an amazing and supernatural experience? Once again, maybe what words cannot explain, my life somehow will.

CHAPTER 22

Leaning on the Everlasting Arms

*T*HE REALITY OF MY SITUATION slapped me in
the face on Monday morning. Phone calls.
Appointments. CT scans. Surgery the following
week to put the port in. Chemo right after that.
Fistful of supplements. New diet. I thought I had
worked through everything, but that day it felt as
if I were starting all over again. It wasn't that I was
afraid or not trusting. The fact that this was *real* hit
me hard that morning. All I could do was sink into
the arms of my Savior and hold on tight! I knew that
was my only safe place.

On Thursday of that week I had surgery to put
in the port and on Friday I had my first chemo treatment. My prayer was that as my family and friends
walked beside me on that journey, God's comfort
would give us all joy. "Your love, Lord, holds me up.
When cares increase within me, your comfort gives
me joy" (Psalm 94:19). On Saturday morning I felt
like I was going to be able to "do this"; on Saturday

afternoon I wasn't so sure. As I was getting ready for Mass, fatigue hit with a vengeance! I have no idea how I made it through that Mass — I didn't have the energy to sit up, much less stand up. Staying focused was just about impossible, and staying awake took all my energy. I slept that evening and most of Sunday, but I was so thankful that nausea wasn't a problem. Monday, however, was a different experience! Nausea hit big-time that morning! I had to take a pill for it, which knocked me out for the rest of the day. About four o'clock in the afternoon I got up for a bit, but all I really wanted to do was sleep! I tried to remember to offer up the crud, but it was hard.

Somehow I did live through those next few days. Nausea, low-grade fever, sweats, raw mouth, achy bones: it was hard to stay positive when I felt so crummy. It seemed like all I did was eat and think about what I could eat next to keep my stomach settled. It wasn't that I was enjoying my food; it was all about trying to feel decent.

There were many things that I had already dealt with: acceptance of the illness, the possibility of death, the loss of my hair, the loss of my life as I knew it. But I discovered that I had to deal with those things over and over again. It was like tuning a violin: you don't tune it once and it's good thereafter. You have to tune it every time you play it, and sometimes you even have to stop in the middle of playing to tune it. So I stopped and faced these issues constantly, and I found myself having to work through things I thought had been dealt with. I had said that I wanted to "do this" well; I discovered that I didn't want to "do this" at all!

By Friday I felt better, my mouth wasn't quite as sore, and I had a little more energy. My friend, Jane, and I sat on our back porch, admiring the progress the landscaper had made on our new, wonderful backyard. I have been so blessed by this woman's friendship! It felt as if she were going through this ordeal with me—the dread, the uncertainties, the feeling bad. Her willingness to share my pain made it easier for me to do what I had to do.

That evening I worked in the food pantry. I was so tired, but working there energized me. I loved being with the volunteers I love so much, the people I had grown to love, doing work that is so satisfying. And being in God's presence in the church filled me with peace and joy and contentment. I couldn't imagine wanting to be anywhere else!

On Saturday night we went to a Fourth of July party. I was surprised at the number of people that knew about the cancer—some I didn't even know; yet they had all been praying for me! As the evening wore on, an interesting thing happened. Instead of getting more tired—as I expected—I became more energized. It seemed like everyone gave me a bit of themselves. Is this how it works? When we share each others' burdens, do they take a little of the suffering upon themselves and give back their energy? Like those who have much share with the poor so they are not in want, so physically and emotionally those who have, give to those in need? I had never thought about exactly how "sharing each others' burdens" worked before then.

I woke up the following Monday morning feeling really good—and really hungry. I was able to eat anything I wanted, and lots of it! Monday afternoon my spiritual director suggested I meditate on Psalm 139. I loved verse 5: "Behind and before you encircle me and rest your hand upon me." I was completely enclosed in Him and wherever I went, He was there with His hand on me, guiding and protecting me. It was the answer to my prayer when I felt so horrible: "Hold me. Please hold me." For several days that was all I could pray, but I knew He was right there with me, holding me through the side effects of the chemo. I love that our great God doesn't make us come to Him; He gladly comes to us if only we ask.

Monday night my girls and several friends came over to watch a movie. They brought soup, fruit, homemade cookies, and spinach-artichoke dip from Olive Garden. I felt like eating pretty much anything, so I really enjoyed the variety. We talked and laughed all through the evening, then Jaime played the piano and Ashley sang for us. It was a perfect evening!

Later that week I meditated some more on Psalm 139, and verses 9 and 10 jumped out at me: "If I fly with the wings of dawn and alight beyond the sea, even there your hand will guide me, your right hand hold me fast." Images of my soaring vision/dream came rushing in. When I'm high above the earth soaring with the eagles, He holds me up and helps me soar. I knew that no matter where that soaring took me, He would be there with me. So beautiful! So comforting!

I had eight more days until I had to do chemo again. I tried not to dread it, but I did. Could I learn to just do what had to be done, suffer the side effects, and not look ahead with dread? It seemed like I should have been able to, but my frail humanity got in the way every time!

God gave me a really good week. I tried to live twice as hard during those good days. Tried to make every minute count twice as much. Tried to let go of anything that kept me from making my life count. I didn't know how much time I had left on this earth, so it was vitally important to accomplish as much as I could with whatever time I had. Having said that, I needed to remember that often the most is accomplished when I just rest with my Savior and don't "try hard" to do it myself! I had restocked the pantry with broth and soup and crackers to get me through another round of yucky nausea. I decided to try taking my nausea medicine early, knowing I'd be completely out of it for a few days. Sleeping had to be better than heaving my guts out!

I realized that I had become comfortable with having cancer and knowing that my time on earth was probably short. It became a part of who I was, just like brown eyes and big feet! It was something to be cherished and embraced. I could sing and rejoice, because this was an important part of my journey, and I wanted to embrace it fully and cheerfully. It was very freeing to accept it so completely. "My eager expectation and hope is that I shall not be put to shame in any way, but that with all boldness, now as always, Christ will be magnified in my body, whether by life or by death" (Philippians 1:20).

Early in the morning we went to the oncologist's for a PET scan, followed by lab work, a visit with the doctor, then my treatment. We arrived at the clinic at 6:30 a.m. and had my port accessed, followed by a finger stick (blood sugar) and dose of radioactive sugar (I think that's what she said). I dozed for about 45 minutes, then they did the PET scan. I had to stay perfectly still for 20 minutes—hard when I needed to sneeze and started to itch. We had a couple of hours for ourselves after that, so we went and had breakfast, then ran a couple of errands. We came back to the clinic, had more blood work done, waited a while for the results of the PET scan, then finally saw the doctor. He said that everything was "squeaky clean." No detectable cancer anywhere.

The trick was the *undetectable* cancer that might have still been in my body. He said our best shot was to treat that aggressively *then*. I asked him what things would look like if the cancer came back. Interesting answer: if there is an isolated tumor somewhere, they can "scoop it out"; otherwise, if it's throughout my body it would be incurable. They could do chemo and radiation, but that would be to hold it at bay as long as possible.

On to the chemo! I had a very painful reaction to one of my medications that morning; my back has never hurt so badly! The nurse was on it immediately: got hot packs for my back; stopped the drip; gave me morphine plus more anti-allergy medicine. It took about 30 minutes (I could be way off there!) for things to settle down; then they continued the drip very slowly. It occurred to me hours later that I never even thought to offer up the pain. I wondered if I could do it after-the-fact!

My Bible reading the next day was in Philippians, and a couple of verses really struck me: "For to you has been granted, for the sake of Christ, not only to believe in him but also to suffer for him" (1:29). And: "I have the strength for everything through him who empowers me" (4:13).

On Saturday afternoon I went to Mass, but I was holding on by a thread. Side effects were kicking in and I was *so tired*. I think I slept about fifteen hours that night—and I was still tired. My teeth were hurting and my mouth was getting really sore. But they gave me different nausea medicine in the hopes that it wouldn't wipe me out so badly, and I hoped that that round of chemo wouldn't be as wicked as the first one had been. But I didn't think I was going to make it through those first few days. The new nausea medicine wasn't as wicked as the first, but I could only take it every eight hours and it seemed to wear off after five or six... I had more flu-like achiness that time around and a wicked, itchy rash broke out on my scalp. The cortisone cream helped... some....

The previous week I had said that I was comfortable with those treatments; could I change my mind? I didn't want to do them anymore! I didn't know if I could get through four more rounds of side effects; I just didn't think I was that strong. I would have loved to have seen some evidence that God was using that misery. Was I so weak and shallow that I needed proof of His working? I hoped not! It would have been an awesome encouragement, though, if I could have.

"Three times I begged the Lord about this, that it might leave me, but He said to me, 'My grace is sufficient for you, for power is made perfect in weakness.' I will rather boast most gladly of my weaknesses, in order that the power of Christ may dwell with me. Therefore, I am content with weakness...

for the sake of Christ; for when I am weak, then I am strong" (2 Corinthians 12:8-10).

The next day went from better, to bad, to worse. I ate way too many wonderful summer tomatoes, and they may have been the cause of my misery. I managed to hang on until evening, but it felt like I had a really bad case of the flu: aches, chills, stomach upset of every kind, debilitating fatigue. About 11:30 p.m., I woke up in desperate pain. I think that was the first time I just really lost it! Cried. Begged God to take this away. Told Him I couldn't do this anymore. And in the quiet hours of the night, He reminded me, "My grace is sufficient." I kept repeating that to myself, knowing it was true, yet still wondering how I could possibly do this four more times.

And the next morning my readings were in 2 Thessalonians: "That our God may make you worthy of his calling and powerfully bring to fulfillment every good purpose and every effort of faith, that the name of our Lord Jesus may be glorified in you..." (1:11-12). He gives me "peace at all times and in every way" (3:16). And 2 Corinthians 12:9: "I will rather boast most gladly of my weaknesses, in order that the power of Christ may dwell in me." So...I didn't know how I was going to get through it. I would try to remember to keep my gaze fixed on Jesus...try to remember to "offer it up"...try to remember to pray, even if it was only, "Hold me,"... try to remember that my family still needed me...

try to remember that God had a purpose in that suffering.

I felt as if I had been the strong one getting my family and friends through that ordeal, but that week there was no strength. I felt weak and defeated, but my weakness was an opportunity for His power. So even when I didn't feel like praying, I trusted God to use each minute as a prayer—a prayer for my family and friends, a prayer for anyone whose life mine touched, however briefly.

CHAPTER 23

Rejoice in the Lord

❀

*O*NE OF THE MOST IMPORTANT LESSONS I've learned as a Catholic Christian is that most things in life are not "either/or," they are "both/and"; not pain *or* joy, but pain *and* joy together. If the threads that make up the fabric of our lives are only pain or only joy, that section of fabric is going to be weak and easily torn, but if we have threads of pain and joy mixed together, then that piece is strong. Being able to accept God's joy in the midst of pain, sorrow, and grief is hard to do, but it is that very gift of God—that we have to open ourselves up to—that makes us strong and witnesses to the world that we are different. It's what our soul yearns for.

I developed a low-grade infection the week after my second treatment and never regained my energy. The doctor changed one of the chemo drugs, hoping to avoid the exceptionally bad side effects the first one had caused. And we made a plan to hopefully avoid more infections by catching any dropping white cell counts more quickly.

But I still dreaded my treatment scheduled for that Friday. With the new drug and new nausea medication, I was hoping things would be better, but at the same time I was afraid to hope. I decided that this time I would offer up the yucks beforehand and ask God to consider it all a prayer. I had learned that there were days I just couldn't pray.

My treatment with the new drugs went uneventfully. I had a nap, a nice visit with the lady beside me, and a foot massage. Later that afternoon I met three of our daughters and my mom at the theater to see *Julie and Julia*; it was probably the best movie I'd seen in a long time. My husband met us for dinner, then I had a good snuggle with our grandbaby before going home and getting to sleep early. All in all, it was a very good day.

The days following that treatment were full of exceptionally hard side effects: nausea, vomiting, bone pain, a rash that itched so bad it woke me up screaming, and—the worst—numb fingers. The side effects were my only reality: I couldn't pray; I couldn't find any joy. And that might have been the most painful thing of all. Was it possible that the joy was still there, all around me like the air I was breathing? Did I have to feel it every moment for it to be the reality of my life? I think my God is bigger than the circumstances of any one day, and I was counting on joy to be a part of that. And is it possible that all of the people who loved me are part of that joy? But early one morning, the Lord brought my own words to me: "Beyond my sight...beyond my feelings...gave me things I couldn't actually feel... it's okay to just 'be.'" Hmmm... Could it be that, like prayer, joy is a bigger part of my life? Even if I couldn't reach out and touch it every minute, could it be a part of who I am? Could my soul be soaring when my body felt grounded? Was there a way to let go of the physical struggle and let Jesus carry me through it to a deeper, more peaceful place? So many questions. So few answers. So, "Could my soul be soaring when my body felt grounded?" I was pretty certain the answer was yes!

I finally felt like reading my morning prayers the following week, and they were all about singing to the Lord with joy. "To you, O God, will I sing a new song, I will play on the ten-stringed harp..." (Psalm 33:2). And "May the God of hope fill you with all joy" (Romans 15:13). Just because I couldn't touch the joy didn't mean it wasn't there!

"Therefore, since we are surrounded by so great a cloud of witnesses" (I thought of all the angels and saints in heaven praying for me), "let us rid ourselves of every burden and sin that clings to us" (show me what they are, Lord), "and persevere in running the race that lies before us" (we don't get to choose it) "while keeping our eyes on Jesus" (Hebrews 12:1-2).

The key to everything was keeping my eyes fixed on Jesus! God had a purpose and it was to "rid (me) of burdens and sins" so that I might finish the race purified and help others to keep their eyes on Jesus as I kept mine on Him. Why He would use me for such a glorious task is beyond me, but I was eager to be used.

And more! "For the sake of the joy that lay before him he endured the cross, despising its shame…" (Hebrews 12:2). Could I paraphrase that? For the sake of the joy that lay before me in heaven, I can endure the chemo and its side effects and whatever may come after that, despising its pain. That might have been taking things too far, and yet I didn't really think so. I had to work through the pain to get to the joy; like having to work through the fear to get to the trust. "My heart is steadfast, God…I will sing and chant praise…. I will praise you among the peoples, Lord; I will chant your praise among the nations" (Psalm 108:1-3). "I rejoice heartily in the Lord, in my God is the joy of my soul…" (Isaiah 61:10).

"Is anyone among you suffering? He should pray. Is anyone in good spirits? He should sing praise" (James 5:13). Going back to Hebrews 12:2: "For the sake of the joy that lay before him he endured the cross, despising its shame…." Was that my answer? That there was a time for everything and that I didn't have to feel the joy in the midst of the suffering, but be content to know it was there—along with the song—when I felt better? What I was beginning to understand is that there are times in our lives that we're incapable of expressing joy, but that doesn't mean it's not there. That was what I had been trying to put my finger on—because I knew the joy had to be there!

Was this the "wrestling with God" our priest had preached on a couple of months before? "To wrestle with someone means you're trying to impose your will on them, and not let them impose their will on you" (Pastor's Pen, July 7, 2009, Father John Antony). Was that what I had been doing? Trying to tell God I didn't want those side effects instead of letting Him use them to teach me what I needed to learn? The idea that God Himself "invites us to wrestle with Him" was a new one to me; it seemed irreverent and sinful! But the more I thought about it, the more I began to grasp the significance (well, at least a little). When you wrestle, you and your opponent are in close contact; not casual contact, but forceful and face-to-face. That's about as close to God as we can get, and yet He invites and encourages us to have that relationship with Him. That pretty much blew *me* away! But—somehow—it's that wrestling that makes us stronger and holier. Did I understand any of that? *No!* But I thought that maybe as I continued to grapple with it, I would start to get a clue. In an odd mix of analogies, I felt like all my cards were on the table, they'd all been wrestled over, and I could enjoy the "cuddle after the wrestle" (e-mail from Father John Antony, August 2009). Father said that just might be what heaven is like. Sometimes he made it hard for me to want to fight the cancer, because why would I want to be anywhere but heaven? He also said God will "dazzle us in heaven" with the ways He has blessed us on earth, that He hides that from us now. What a great thought, that God will dazzle us!! He does a good job of that now; I can only imagine (well, I can't actually) what more He will do in heaven.

I saw my doctor again and, once more, we decided to change one of my drugs, hoping to avoid so many side effects. He offered me three choices, one of which was to stop chemotherapy at that point. I was so, so tempted. But I think that if the cancer ever came back, I needed to know that I had given it my best shot. I didn't want any of us to have to look back and wonder "if only."

I had a tough realization the following week: I was trying to do too much, trying to do things I shouldn't have been doing, and trying to do things too soon after my treatments. I kept thinking that because I had ten good days after the first round of chemo I should have them every time, and I planned my days accordingly. So my new plan was not to expect to feel good, and if I did, then I would make plans. But really, I had enough with choir, piano, organ, and writing. I decided that friends could stop in for a visit, but I wasn't going to try to meet them out for lunch anymore. I enjoyed visiting with them, but going out took everything out of me. I realized that if I had to push to do something, then it was probably too much. Duh…it was just really hard for me to accept that I couldn't do the things I wanted to do!

I had my fourth treatment at the end of August— the first with the new drug. It went uneventfully, but nausea started setting in by dinner time; I hoped the medicine would keep it from becoming unbearable.

I decided that it was time to stop and count my many blessings instead of dwelling on how wretched I felt.

1. God blessed me with great parents. Parents that loved me, cared for me, and taught me about Jesus' love at an early age. My mom continues to be my greatest supporter and prayer warrior.

2. God has blessed me with almost 41 years with the most wonderful, loving husband. I'm a better person for having been loved by him. I couldn't ask for anything more.

3. God blessed us with six wonderful children. They have grown into adults that are fun to be with, who are kind and loving, and who live their faith. I couldn't be more blessed.

4. God has blessed us with six grandchildren who fill our days with joy. Watching them grow brings such happiness to our lives.

5. God has blessed us with amazing friends. Friends who aren't afraid to "speak the truth in love" (Ephesians 4:15). Friends who are trying to grow in their faith and live and share that faith. Friends who are always there.

6. God has blessed us in ways we could never have imagined when He brought us home to the Catholic Church. He has poured out His great mercy on us, taught us to trust Him complete, taught us how to listen to His still, quiet voice, taught us what it means to give Him everything that we have and everything that we are. I could write an entire book on how He has used the Catholic Church as a vehicle for His blessings.

7. God gave me ten glorious days in Hawaii with my wonderful husband *before* we found the cancer. Water. Sand. Sunshine. Whales. Sunsets. Sunrises. A slice of heaven on earth.

8. He let me sing Brahms' "Requiem" just before my diagnosis, and, Lord willing, I will get to sing the full-length Handel's "Messiah" for Christmas this year.

9. All the food pantry volunteers have been such a blessing. They pitched in and kept the food pantry running without a hitch in my absence. What great people!

10. So...I could have kept counting, but for that day, I decided I'd covered a good portion of my blessings. But there was one last blessing: God has used my cancer and its treatments (in spite of my whining about the side effects) to teach me lessons I could not have learned any other way, to draw me close to His Heart, to show me how many wonderful people love me, to teach me how to cherish every moment. What a priceless gift!

"The God of all grace who called you to his eternal glory through Christ Jesus will himself restore, confirm, strengthen, and establish you after you have suffered a little" (1 Peter 5:10).

CHAPTER 24

Wings as Eagles

THE FIRST WEEK OF SEPTEMBER was one I wished I could have forgotten. It had been a discouraging, emotional, and weepy week. Early in the week it had seemed as if things weren't going to be so bad, and in some ways they weren't: I didn't have the bone pain or the mouth sores or a rash, but when the nausea kicked in, it did it with a vengeance. I'm afraid I didn't handle it well at all! I was feeling really alone and terribly isolated. I knew that I was surrounded by prayer, but I still felt alone in the suffering—no one else could do that for me. No one else could feel the complete discouragement or the debilitating nausea and misery. I knew the next week would be better (at least I hoped it would be better!) and I would feel more connected, but that knowledge didn't make that current one any easier to bear.

My sister told me that she suspected the chemo had been a lot harder on me than I had expected it to be, and she was right. I had an image of myself as strong enough to handle anything, and I discovered that these bones are just crumbling dust! And while my spirit was good, the impact on my emotions began to take its toll. Like my body, my emotions were far more fragile than I would have liked. But all of this reminded me of my frail humanity; I was not, nor would I ever be, a superwoman. For some reason I had always felt like I should be able to be that strong, energetic, do-everything-that-needs-to-be-done kind of person. Did that come from having raised a large family? From our culture? From my ingrained personality? Once again the why was less important than coming face-to-face with the fact that I am only one human, with very human limitations. Did any of this help me cope with the debilitating misery and emotional collapse that was my lot? Probably not, but it at least reminded me that my expectations needed to be based on the facts at hand and not on unrealistic fantasies.

On Tuesday I finally thought I might make it. I was still tired and the queasiness came and went, but at least I could do a few of the activities I wanted and needed to do. I woke up early that morning with some interesting thoughts on my mind. I was still chewing on the "wrestling with God" homily and realized that the struggle I was having with my expectations was wrestling with God big time!

I *wanted* to let go of it, but I just couldn't seem to be able to.

I also felt that God was preparing me for round number five of chemo to be really hard. I couldn't imagine it being any harder than the last one had been, but there it was. When I was so physically and emotionally drained, how could I prepare myself to do it again? I really wished I knew!

If dread is a sin then I was in trouble, because I can't begin to tell you how much I dreaded those last two treatments. Once again, God reminded me that I could soar. (Was I soaring? It certainly didn't feel like it!) And I could see the rogue wave coming toward me. I couldn't get far enough out to sea to ride over the top, and I was too far out to make it back to shore. (And actually I think it would have been a sin to try!) I thought it would just swallow me up, and I wasn't sure what to do until it hit. I think I was back to fighting my way through the fear to get to the trust. Had I been wrong? Could I have fear and trust at the same time? Just then it felt like it might be possible! Then I decided that maybe it wasn't so much fear as dread, and I was quite certain that dread and trust could coexist.

Part of my reading that morning was Psalm 86:12-13, and those lines so expressed what was in my heart: "I will praise you with all my heart, glorify your name forever, Lord my God. Your love for me is great." I had asked God at the very beginning of my diagnosis to use it and me to bring glory to His name and to make a difference in peoples' lives. How He could use such a fragile, whining, emotional and physical wreck to do that was beyond me, and yet He had shown me over and over that He had.

The next three days were crazy! I had been running a temperature when I went for my organ lesson on Thursday morning and it was still high when I finished. I should have been more prepared for the nurse's reaction: "Come straight to the office." My blood counts were completely out-of-whack, with almost no white blood cells. Nurses immediately swarmed around me, put a mask on my face, hooked up IV antibiotics, and gave me a long list of "dos and don'ts" when my counts were low. I also got a shot of Neupogen to help boost those white cells. (They only tell you how bad that shot is going to sting just as they are ready to stick!!) There would be more shots on Friday and Saturday.

The nurses told me that I could have a long-ago planned luncheon at my house on Friday, but I would have to wear a mask and be scrupulous about hand washing and germs. I woke up Friday feeling a bit better and really looking forward to having our church staff at our house for lunch. I had put chicken in the crock pot the night before and everyone else brought all the side dishes we needed to make tacos. All in all it was two hours of *pure joy*! So while I may have taken a big risk physically, I was in much better spirits for it.

After lunch we went back to the doctor's office for my second shot of Neupogen and were (again) totally unprepared for what we got. My temp was pretty high, my heart rate very high. So...another round of antibiotics in addition to the shot. Saturday morning I went for round three of antibiotics and a shot and was told I couldn't leave my house that weekend. I had so been looking forward to Mass that afternoon.

We had been planning a trip to New York for the following weekend. Our son was coming home from Iraq and *nothing* was going to keep me from being there and getting my arms around him! But I had been so sick, I didn't know if I was going to get to go. On Monday morning I woke up feeling much better. My blood counts were good and I was given permission to travel on Friday. I was a very happy mom!

I had made a list of things that I really wanted to do once that year was behind me:

1. Go to Hawaii with my husband
2. Take my mom to Missouri to do some family research
3. Go to Disney World with my sister
4. Sing in the chorale at the university
5. Play the piano
6. Learn to play the organ

It was hard for me to see where the energy was going to come from to actually *do* those things. I was so weary from all the surgeries and the chemo, and I knew I would be tired during the radiation as well. Would I ever feel like "me" again? Or was that bone-weary emptiness what I would live with for the rest of my life? I discovered (again) that acceptance was a key issue for me. Accepting the cancer, and even that my life could be cut short: not a problem. Accepting how I felt during those treatments and resenting not being able to live my life fully: big problem. The thing was, I never could figure out how to accept it.

A very wise priest posed this question to me: "What are you afraid of losing?" My mind chewed on that one for hours! When I was so miserable and sick, and my emotions were shot, there just didn't seem to be any room for God, and that was devastating! Father explained to me that darkness teaches us to love God for Who He is, not for the consolations He gives us. So somehow, even when I felt spiritually empty, God was still at work in my soul, teaching me to love Him wholly and getting rid of anything that came between us. I also learned that expectations revolved around me: what *I* wanted; what made *me* feel useful and fulfilled; what made *me* feel like I had accomplished something. So when I *expected* to feel good "tomorrow," that was so I could do what was important to *me*. But when I *hoped* tomorrow would be better, that connected me with God and opened the way for Him to accomplish *His* purpose for my day. So I knew and could accept that *whatever* the day would bring was part of His plan for my life, and I could be content with that.

One last thing: Father told me that when the rogue wave hit, I could quote Jesus' words on the Cross and say, "Into Your hands I commend my spirit." I didn't have to *do* anything to get ready for it, I didn't have to try to outrun it, ride over it, or swim through it. I just had to give myself to God and trust Him to bring me safely through, in whatever form that would take.

I woke up at two o'clock Friday morning with a clear answer to the question, "What am I holding on tight to?" He showed me that I was clinging to what I wanted my days to be like, instead of accepting what He brought to me each day. (You might have noticed a recurring theme here!) I was clinging to my life as I knew it, and I needed the grace (lots and lots of it!) to let go of my old life and embrace the new one God had prepared for me. I didn't know what that would look like and I was a little afraid, but I knew that whatever God had waiting for me could only be good. And I wanted the peace that Father talked about. Boy, did I want that peace! Could I still feel sad about losing my life? I didn't know. Was there a way to feel sadness and joy at the same time over losing things I loved? I didn't know that either. All I really knew for certain was that I wanted to do what God wanted me to do. I wanted my life to glorify His Holy Name. I wanted my life to make a difference in this world. I guess I had my own ideas about how to do that and it was time for me to put more actions to my words and give up my life for His life, my heart for His heart. And really, what more could I want? But it was still hard, and I was not certain how long it would take me to loosen my grasp and totally let go. I knew for certain that He would help me do it in His time.

I received a note from my sister that week:

Dear Rob,

About those expectations…I was thinking that growing up in church we learned (I did, anyway) to handle life "with God's help" — which still leaves things in our hands rather that His ("when you reach the end of your rope, tie a knot,"…that sort of thing). It's all me-centered and based on our own strength. We therefore expect to be able to handle anything "with God's help."

But sometimes life gets really tough and we have absolutely no strength of our own. Maybe it takes really difficult circumstances to make us let go of that rope and just fall into our Father's hands. It's really all about Him and His strength — it's not about me. Even though I've grown past that belief (and I think you have too),

it's still hiding out deep in our hearts and
pops up sometimes — making us feel that
we need to do something instead of just
being still and knowing that He is God.
Just a thought,
Much love — Nancy

My friends and family told me (sometimes indirectly) that the goal was to survive the cancer. I think, rather, that the goal was to learn the lessons I needed to learn, to grow ever closer to my loving Savior, and to willingly bow to His will. Those were hard lessons, but when I finally learned them, the prize would be worth any amount of grief and loss and suffering. I just prayed that I would learn what I was supposed to learn, and ultimately that I could be an instrument of His love and grace on this earth.

I *did* get to go to New York to see our son. We drove three days in the truck, towing his car. I learned an important lesson on that trip: when you have chemo fog where your brain used to be is not the best time to interpret directions and maps and be the navigator! While I didn't get us terribly lost, we did take the scenic rather than the most direct route a couple of times. I'm sure Ken was frustrated with me, but he handled it with grace and humor. When we got to New York we had one day of waiting in the hotel, then *finally* got to go to the airfield for the wel-come-home ceremony. I don't think there was a dry eye in the house when they announced the opening of the ceremony. The band played. The hangar door went up and there stood our soldiers in formation with the sun setting behind them. Very, very emotional! We spent two wonderful days sightseeing and hanging out with him, and then we had to head home. We drove 1305 miles in two days, and I woke up with a miserable cold the next day.

Well...the cold turned into a mild case of pneumonia. I wasn't feeling well on Wednesday when I picked our daughter up at the airport. She and I went to Walmart to buy food for the food pantry, and I was feeling way more tired than before, (grammar...I know) but I thought dinner would pick me up. We went to the steakhouse and I ordered salmon; it tasted good (everything seemed really salty, though) and I was able to eat a fair amount of it. But, honestly, I didn't think I could get myself to the car when we finished. I just wanted to lie down on the bench and sleep. We did get home, but everything hurt and I was feeling queasy; it was hard to breathe and I developed a dry cough that really, really hurt. My family ended up taking me to the ER; the doctor said it wasn't full-blown pneumonia, but it *was* pneumonia. Our daughter, who has had way too much experience with it, said she thinks it would have been full-blown by morning if it hadn't been treated that night.

After a few days I got better, but the coughing *hurt,* and, in spite of medicine, I was still coughing a lot. The hardest part of all of that was that I was not allowed to leave home until after I finished my last chemo. I missed Mass. I missed my friends. I missed singing. I couldn't shop for things I *needed.* (I know there is Internet shopping, but how do you find jeans that fit if you don't try them on?) It was so frustrating! I might have been able to do a few things if I wore a mask. But how humiliating was that? And was my family *really* going to let me, even then? I didn't think so.

I tried to tell myself that there were plenty of things to do while I was at home alone: reading, writing, playing the piano, typing my manuscript. The problem was, I just didn't feel like doing those things much of the time. I was hoping I could practice the organ alone in the church a fair bit. I did love that! I wished I felt like sewing curtains and decorating. And I really thought I'd while away some time scrapbooking and making Scripture cards, but none of that happened.

So...I got to practice letting go of my old life and accepting what each day brought as a gift from God. It was so easy to forget that part; whatever He sent was for my best, however hard it was. I discovered that it was one thing to accept suffering as a theory, but actually living through the nuts and bolts of it was a lot harder; I tried to be more open to the graces

God sent down to get me through it, and I needed to remember to offer it up. That was easy to remember before and after, but in the middle of the trial I really needed someone to remind me. I tried to accept that as God's plan for those weeks, but that acceptance was a struggle. I thought back on Father's homily on what it means to wrestle with God. I'm still not at all sure I understand that concept, but I think I'm getting to practice it. It's like algebra used to be for me: I really didn't understand what I was doing, but somehow I always (well, almost) got the right answer. So maybe the doing would eventually help me understand the end result of this wrestle. (Did that make any sense?) A verse in 1 Samuel caught my attention that morning: "Stand ready to witness the great marvel the LORD is about to accomplish before your eyes" (12:16). I was waiting anxiously to see that great marvel!

CHAPTER 25

The Way of the Cross

B Y OCTOBER I WAS FEELING MUCH BETTER. Still coughing, but not quite as hard and it didn't hurt quite as much. I was still tired but could at least do a little before I wore out. I dreaded Thursday's treatment more than I could say. It felt as if I were ready to start the hardest part of the climb up the mountain. I also had the gut feeling that those last two treatments were going to be worse than anything I'd experienced up to that point. I wondered that I got to see *all* of our children the week before the treatment, and I really wasn't sure the pneumonia was far enough behind me to do it again, but I was going to trust my doctor with that call.

I got to finish the "letting go" discussion with Father on Thursday morning before my treatment. I was hoping he could help me figure out how to do that; the peace he said would come with that "letting go" was not with me. It seemed like it should have been such a simple thing; after all it was what I

150

wanted to do! But I discovered that wanting to let go, knowing how to let go, and actually letting go were three very different things. I thought I had loosened my grasp on parts of my old life, and then realized that I was holding on tighter than ever. I was sure that when the time was right God would give me the grace I needed to "let go of the rope and fall into His loving arms."

In spite of all my struggles and frailties, I still asked God to use those circumstances, to use me, to make a difference in this world, to encourage others, and to bring glory to His Holy Name, because, in the end, that was my prayer and my desire. So I hoped that God would honor my heart and help me soar through the rest of those treatments.

I was sitting in my recliner in the chemo room, waiting for my drugs to be delivered and hooked up. The visit with the doctor had been interesting. He said that I made him nervous because I had been sick so much. I think that if I had said I wanted to discontinue the chemo he would have agreed. But I got a shot of Neulasta the next day to boost white blood cell counts, hoping to get a jump on my immune system. We decided to do my last treatment in two weeks instead of three. It was going to be pretty rough, but we hoped that I would feel good for my birthday party the next month, and then that chapter of my life could be behind me.

I had another discussion with Father that morning. He said that all the good things we do—going to Mass, reading the Bible, making music, being with family and friends—are a bridge to God, but they are not God. He said we get very comfortable on the bridge, but the time comes to leave the bridge and come face-to-face with God Himself. So even if I couldn't go to Mass or read my Bible, I could still have the God of the Mass and the God of the Bible. He's all mine.

We talked about letting go of the things I'm attached to. He said I didn't have to let go of the *thing*, just the attachment to the thing! I was able to do that with our house; so surely He would help me do it with these activities that comprised my life, and I didn't have to do it all at once. I told him that this felt different than leaving our old church and having our life taken from us; this felt like voluntarily giving things up. Father asked me if I didn't think my life had been taken from me then, too. I guess realistically it had. I couldn't do any of the things that used to make up my life, and it certainly revolved around doctor's appointments, ER runs, and how I felt. It didn't feel like much of a life at all, but if that's the one God gave me then I needed to learn to be content with it. I guessed it was just God and me, and that was all I wanted—all I needed. Getting there had been a struggle I didn't even realize I was having. But it's always interesting to see how God had been working in my soul when I had been busy "doing" other things.

I thought about the possibility of getting to sing Handel's "Messiah" that year and realized it might be good to let go of that dream. I had a feeling that if I hung on to it I might not be able to sing, but if I could let go of it maybe God would give it back to me. That would be such a gift!

I also decided to make a list of spiritual lessons I had learned that year. The two most impressive to my soul were, "You don't have to lose the *thing*, just the attachment to it," and, "Maybe it's time to leave the bridge behind and just be with God." Powerful, powerful concepts. When I considered that God had brought me to that place—spiritually and to the Catholic Church—before He let me have cancer, I was overwhelmed with gratitude. I couldn't imagine a pastor in any previous church spending so much time helping me work through the spiritual issues that presented themselves, and having a spiritual director that helped me explore those issues was a double blessing.

I finally made peace with the side effects. The week after my fifth treatment, I was able to simply rest and accept feeling yucky; I didn't even think about all the things I wished I could be doing. I thought my soul had at last found that quiet, peaceful resting place.

I tried to share with my spiritual director how devastating the dark, lonely, numb place I felt stuck in was. (I think *that* was the harder circumstances after the fifth and sixth chemo treatments.) I hadn't been able to feel God's presence for several weeks. He had always been so close, so to lose that closeness felt like the worst thing that could happen. How could I do this without Him? How could I "leave the bridge" if He wasn't there? I felt caught between the darkness and the nothingness, with no way out. Had the physical, mental, emotional, and spiritual onslaughts of the past few months all come crashing down on me? But in the silence God told me that was where I needed to be! My mind could not even go there, but I totally trusted Him. If He was using me, even in that pit, then that was where I wanted to be. Knowing that I was where He wanted me to be gave me peace amidst the loneliness and numbness and darkness.

Our daughter and I planted tulips in our new garden that October. I had been feeling alone and disconnected; I knew that I was surrounded with prayers and love from everyone, but I just couldn't seem to connect to it in any way. As I was digging the hole and pushing my tulip bulb into it, I realized that it has to be in the ground, in the dark, for a season before it can burst into the sunlight and bloom into the beautiful flower that it is. And I wondered if my life was like that just then. If maybe I needed to be "in the dark," alone and disconnected, for a season before I could feel the sunshine again and before I could bloom.

We geared up for another week of side effects. I hoped I could keep that newly found peace with them! Sometime toward the end of the year we would do a PET scan to see where things stood. I thought it might be hard for me to figure out how to live after that. Would I always wonder if or when the cancer might come back? That was probably the learning to take life one day at a time and not worrying about tomorrow. Oh — so hard for me! I like to have a plan and know what's coming!! And yet I'm so grateful I can't see what's coming before it gets here. God is good to give us one day at a time.

That week I received another note from my sister:

Rob — Isn't it interesting how God gave
you the tulip picture just when you needed
it? I'll need to give that one some thought
since I'm going through a stretch where I
just don't feel God answering my prayers
and I'm feeling rather abandoned too. Yet I
know (in my head) that He's there and He
cares just like you know (in your head) that
all of us who love you are out here praying
for you even when you feel disconnected.

As for living with the fear that the
cancer will return...I think it's like living
in California. You know an earthquake

can happen — and they do from time to
time — but you don't live your life worry-
ing about it, which would cripple you.
          ☺ *Love you — Nan*

A friend came to eat lunch with me one day
that week. What a treat! We sat on the bed and ate
our lunches and talked and giggled like teenagers.
Talked about girl stuff like pedicures and grandba-
bies. For an hour we didn't talk about cancer at all.
Those small, normal-life stuff became the greatest
blessings.

At the end of October, I shared this letter:

To my faithful family and friends,

    This has been an odd post-chemo week.
The nausea, for the most part, hasn't been
too bad. And I've craved — and eaten — weird
things like steak and tacos and corn dogs.
(Real nutritious — I know!) I ran a rather
high fever early in the week, and there's
a mystery pain in my back. But, in spite
of all that, as long as I kept still, I didn't
feel too bad. Yesterday and today I've been
able to be up and even get out a bit. I'm so
looking forward to picking up the pieces of
my life again. I'll need to go slowly and be
sure I only do what God wants me to do.
More hard lessons to learn, because as my
friends, you know I want to do everything!

*I'd like to share a paragraph from
my book. These words were written
long before we knew we would be facing
this battle, but I go to them frequently
for encouragement. I hope you will
also find encouragement in them.*

*"Since my Confirmation, my life is and
has been marked by a settledness, a sureness
that I had never known before. I feel the
power of the presence of the Holy Spirit in
my days; I've been marked with the stamp
of God's all-consuming love. My prayer is
that that power, that love will pour out of
me into every person I touch as I live this
life God has given me, that He will use me
to make a difference in this world. My life
has certain purpose as I live my days — no
more coasting along or floundering. I am
strong, as I know I can face anything; I
can do anything God asks of me, because
I have His constant nourishment and
protection. And while it's difficult to put
into words the effect my Confirmation
has had on me, I trust that what words
can't explain, my life somehow will."*

Much love,

Robbie

I was still struggling with the idea of "leaving the bridge behind" if I couldn't connect to God's presence when I got to the other side. I knew He was there; He had promised He would never leave me. Sometimes I started feeling insecure and wondered if I had done something to be in that situation or if there was something I needed to do to get out of that empty place. I decided that was probably the "old me" feeling like that; I had never heard of darkness like that. I had only known about spiritual darkness from not knowing God. Two entirely different things!!

A new idea occurred to me: God didn't have to be using me. The fact that He was working *in me*, changing me was enough. In the midst of waiting — of being — God was accomplishing things in me.

"Fear not, for I have redeemed you; I have called you by name: you are mine. When you pass through the water, I will be with you; in the rivers you shall not drown. When you walk through fire, you shall not be burned; the flames shall not consume you. For I am the Lord, your God, the Holy One of Israel, your savior" (Isaiah 43:1-3). I trusted in that promise to see me through. I had been in the river and in the fire before in my life, and I came through them stronger and happier. I rested in that hope again.

CHAPTER 26

Only Trust Him

I NEEDED TO TALK TO SOMEONE about the empty disconnect I was feeling. I went through the motions of living and being with people, but it felt as if I were not in my body. I wondered, "If it isn't me, then who is it?" Even when I went to the chapel and to Mass, it just didn't *feel* like I was there. I prayed, I listened, but it felt like my prayers just echoed back to me. I felt so alone in that dark place! Was that how Jesus felt on the Cross—abandoned by His Father? I just couldn't understand. Had I done something? Not done something? Was it a physical thing from my body being so abused by chemo drugs? Other than my spiritual director and our priest, I didn't feel I could share that strange place I was in. I wished I could.

"Lord, I just want to feel your presence around me and in me again! I need You so much! I know You're there, but I can't feel Your presence. Is this soaring? It doesn't feel like it! I feel as if I've crashed into the side of a cliff and fallen mortally wounded to the ground. And no one even knows I'm here" (Journal entry, November 16, 2009).

My Tuesday morning reading expressed so much of what I was feeling those days! "How long, Lord? Will you utterly forget me? How long will you hide your face from me? How long must I carry sorrow in my soul, grief in my heart day after day?… Look upon me, answer me, Lord, my God!… [but as for me] I trust in your faithfulness…that I may sing of the Lord, 'How good our God has been to me!'" (Psalm 13:1-3, 5-6).

"Blessed is the man who trusts in the Lord, whose hope is the Lord. He is like a tree planted beside the water; that stretches out its roots to the stream: It fears not the heat when it comes, its leaves stay green; In the year of the drought it shows no distress, but still bears fruit" (Jeremiah 17:7-8). I wanted to think that in that "drought" I was still bearing fruit! But I really hoped my "year of drought" would be behind me soon! I wished there were something I could do to bring the rain and the sunshine!! I felt so alone…so empty. But even in spite of the pain and the emptiness, I was not sad! God had given me a cheerful spirit in the midst of that darkness, and I was so thankful for that.

My husband and I had birthdays coming up, and I decided that it was a good time to ponder the precious life God had given me. Every day was a gift to be treasured and lived fully. It was also a good time to consider what is truly important in this life: faith, family, and friends gets it for me. Living my days to reflect those things can sometimes be a challenge; it's easy for me to get in the way of my own good intentions!

I decided to make a list of spiritual lessons I had learned. Not mastered, but at least learned.

1. God reveals Himself to us in ways we could never imagine.
2. When we ask God to use us to bring Him glory, He will! But probably in ways we didn't anticipate.
3. God is always in the silence.
4. The power of the Holy Spirit is a very concrete thing.
5. God prepares the way for us, but we have to be paying attention!
6. God knows what He is doing.
7. Take things one day at a time.
8. Life is rarely either/or. It's usually both/and.
9. God's strength shines through my weakness.
10. God's grace is sufficient.
11. Offer it up!
12. God is always worthy of praise, not the circumstances.
13. Life is all about waiting.
14. God gives the most amazing peace in the midst of trial.

15. I will always be *me*! Not cancer, not treatments, not side effects, not the things I do. It's easy to feel like I become those things, but I am still the same person God created.
16. God fights for us and gives us victory.
17. Trusting God is always my choice.
18. Our lives touch others in ways we can never know or imagine.
19. Even cancer is a gift.
20. I usually have to work through things more than once!
21. God loves me more than my human mind can comprehend.
22. God's comfort brings joy.
23. It's okay — even good — just to "be."
24. We do not get to choose the course set before us; God chooses it for us.
25. I need to let go of anything that comes between God and me.
26. God gives us glimpses of heaven if we just keep our eyes open.
27. Suffering is a gift.
28. Even when I can't pray, my *life* can still be a prayer.
29. I cannot trust my feelings to understand the reality.
30. Expectations are about me, while hope is about God.

31. Darkness teaches us to love God for Who He is, not for what He gives us.
32. He always sends us the grace to do what He's asked us to do.
33. God can use me even when I don't feel like doing anything.
34. God gives me a bit of Himself in my family and friends.
35. God loves it when I praise Him!
36. We don't have to let go of the *thing*, just the *attachment* to the thing.
37. God is all I want. All I need.
38. God *does* speak to us when we're willing to listen.
39. Joy does not come from circumstances or possessions; it comes from our heavenly Father.
40. Every day is a gift from God to be treasured and lived fully.

Our priest assured me that "God *is* present! God *is* using me! I can't soar all the time. My wings have been clipped for a time, but God can use me even when I'm grounded; people still see God and sense His presence in me" (Journal entry, December 1, 2009). Can I be content to be a channel of God's love without feeling His presence? Can knowing that others are seeing God in me be enough? My focus had to be holiness and loving God — not how I felt!

Tuesday was mostly a good day: I spent time with the neighborhood ladies (they don't come any better!); bought rice and meat for the food pantry; practiced the organ; had radiation; shopped for Christmas decorations; saw *The Blindside* with Ken; ate pizza for supper; decorated the mantel; then got so sick I wanted to die. Everything hurt. I was completely worn out. I had really overdone it.

Spiritually…oh, boy. That dark, empty hole I was in remained as dark and empty as ever. I *knew* God was with me and used me to show His presence to others. I needed to focus more on that and less on how I felt.

I saw our family doctor that week to check thyroid levels and to start nutrient IVs. He said an interesting thing: "When I look at your face (and I thought, 'Uh-oh, what does he see?') I see a serenity I don't see in cancer patients." Wow. Could people really see God's presence in my face, in my life?

So I was challenged to see God's presence around me — the garden, music, people, clouds…. I could *see* Him in those things, but I still couldn't *feel* Him in those things. At the same time — this seemed contradictory, and yet it wasn't — I was completely surrounded by and saturated with the most amazing peace. Maybe I could learn to feel His presence in that peace. Maybe I could feel His presence after all, just not in the ways I had come to know.

On Friday I rested. I had radiation that afternoon, but I was saving all my energy for singing Handel's "Messiah": rehearsal that night, then performances on Saturday and Sunday. It would be very hard to describe the place I was in that weekend. As I sang "Messiah" I felt as if I had been caught up in the peace and transported to heaven. It definitely felt like soaring! I decided that maybe I could get used to soaring days interspersed with grounded days. If I could just learn to take those days as they came, and not waste my energy wishing they were different; to be content even with dark, empty, lonely days; to look for the reality instead of focusing on how I felt—could God just soak into my being and replace me with Him?

The next week was full. They scheduled a CT scan, a PET scan, and an appointment with the doctor. I had radiation every day, music lessons, food pantry, spiritual direction. My biggest problem was finding the silence and stillness I was craving. I tried to live a normal, albeit ridiculously busy, life that week, but it felt good to be living again instead of just passing the time. By seven that evening (or three o'clock!) I was exhausted and ready for bed, but at least I had earned that exhaustion.

That cloud of peace still surrounded me. While I would have liked to just sit and savor God's presence in that peace, I had a life to be living. I didn't know how God used those days, but I was quite certain that He did; I was content to live out my days and let Him figure out the plan. I loosened up a lot that year when it came to scheduling my days and wanting to control my life. I didn't know that was a lesson I so desperately needed to learn.

Spiritually, I was feeling very settled. I didn't have much to say to God; I was just content to feel His presence. It definitely felt like the "snuggle after the wrestle" — content and peaceful. Emotionally, things were great. Mentally, I wished I had my brain back. Physically, I thought things were good. I went hard through the day, then slept hard — and for a long time — at night.

I was down to six more days of radiation! One full dose, then five aimed only at the three tumor sites. My skin was starting to split, and it really did hurt. That whole quadrant of my body was so tender and sore. The other weird thing was that I'd been running a pretty high fever in the evenings. I didn't feel sick; I wondered if it was an effect of the radiation. I would be so glad when that ordeal was over, and my very frail humanity sincerely hoped I would never have to go through it again. I thought I'd just have to curl up and die; couldn't even think about getting through that torture again. I decided I'd gotten through the crisis and then I fell apart. It had nothing to do with faith or trust or spirituali-ty — I was just physically and emotionally used up.

I still felt pretty disconnected from everything and everyone. I went through all the motions of living, but it still felt as if I weren't in my body. It was a hard thing to describe. The dark place I was in was different those days. I *could* feel God's presence in the peace that surrounded me—and I was so thankful for that! I could see Him all around me—and I was thankful for that. But I couldn't seem to feel *close* to God. Why? When that's what I wanted more than anything, why wasn't that closeness there? Was it me? Had I done—or not done—something? Or was this part of His being there beyond my perception? I needed to learn to be faithful and trust Him even without feeling Him so close. Those were hard lessons to learn. Hard lessons to understand. I begged the Lord to help me stay faithful to Him, to help me learn to love Him completely, to help me abandon myself to His will.

I needed to let go of as much as I possibly could. I thought that instead of trying to detach and gain holiness, I needed to let go and allow God to do it for me. I needed to just "be." Very, very hard for me. "Love God" requires being, but "love neighbor" requires a lot of work. Hmm…

In mid-December I sent this letter to my family and friends:

Dear Family and Friends,

This will be my final Friday report. My scans this week show no detectable cancer in my body. I have two-and-a-half weeks of radiation, one more nutrient IV, and a minor surgery to remove the port; then I will be finished with treatment. And while my journey through life will continue, at least this chapter of it is coming to a close. It has been a chapter I never expected to live, nor one I would have chosen for myself. But it's a chapter I am extremely grateful for! I've learned lessons about myself and about God that I never could have learned any other way. His mercy and faithfulness have sustained me through the circumstances of the year. When I thought I couldn't go on, He was always there to carry me through it. I've learned that trusting God is always my choice, but when I do, He blesses me beyond my imagination. And, in the final analysis, I've learned that God is all I need.

I think I might have a better handle on living one day at a time, taking life as it comes instead of trying to engineer it to fit my preconceived ideas of how it should be. I see each new day as a gift: one to be fully lived and cherished. And while I feel an urgency to live every day to its fullest, I also crave time to be quiet, to just "be." Time to rest, to pray, to ponder God's goodness.

You have all been such an encouragement and blessing. You've helped me see things from a perspective I often didn't have. You've shared your thoughts and your hearts with me. God used

you to help carry me over the rough
spots. You are all very dear to me.

    So, as this journey and this year come to
a close, I pray for a joyous Christmas and a
very blessed New Year for each one of you.
"To the one who is able to keep you from
stumbling and to present you unblemished
and exultant, in the presence of his glory,
to the only God, our Savior, through Jesus
Christ our Lord be glory, majesty, power,
and authority from ages past, now, and
for ages to come. Amen" (Jude 1:24-25).

        Merry Christmas,
        Robbie

So…on January 2, 2010, I thought maybe I was through with that particular journal. For then, at least, I was cancer-free and ready to live hard. I had much to do in 2010; I just needed to learn to balance the quiet and the doing and learn to take life one day at a time. I had a 28% chance of cancer reappearing in the next two years. I couldn't get caught up in thinking it *would* come back, but, on the other hand, I needed to be realistic about knowing it was a very real possibility. My life was in God's hands; He could do with me whatever He willed. So…cancer, no cancer, being, doing, tired, energetic, alone, working…whatever circumstance I was in, my life's priority had to be to pray, adore, love, worship God, and to strive for holiness in my life and love for my neighbor. I would try to let go of all expectation and let *God* do His work in me; I just needed to be receptive to His life in me and respond to life as He wished. Sounded like a life-long project to me!

PART III

Learning to Live: Prayer

CHAPTER 27

Pass Me Not

STRUGGLED FOR MONTHS TRYING to understand this dark, lonely, empty hole I felt stuck in... couldn't escape from. Where was God? I *knew* He was there—He had promised never to leave me (Deuteronomy 31:6)—but I couldn't sense His presence. I tried to pray, but it felt like empty words bouncing off the walls. I went to Mass, but it felt like motions without meaning. I read my Bible, but it felt like blank pages staring back at me.

I began to be really afraid that, somehow, God had left me, abandoned me. In my heart of hearts I knew that wasn't possible, but that's how it felt. My priest and spiritual director both assured me that at the right time, God would free me from the darkness and bring me into His light. I tried to be content in my little dark hole and rest in God's perfect timing for the sunshine. Eventually the fear of the darkness left me, but intense loneliness remained. The one thing I wanted was God, and it seemed like that's the one thing I couldn't have. I felt alone, and I was devastated. I cried to God with a longing, a yearning I had never known before. I was grief-stricken. I wondered if the trauma of the past year had emptied me completely—physically *and* spiritually. I wondered if, as my body healed, my spirit might also heal. Yet, in spite of that empty, disconnected, dark place where I was very much alone, I was aware of God's amazing peace surrounding me, saturating me, dwelling in me. I couldn't feel *God*, but I could feel *His peace*. It sounds like it should be a great contradiction, and yet it felt perfectly right. It was the "peace that passes all understanding" (Philippians 4:7).

In January of that year I had the opportunity to go on another directed silent retreat. I had looked forward to it for months, for I felt certain that I would finally hear God's voice, see God's hand at work, feel His presence, but it turned out to be the most miserable weekend of my life! For me, He was nowhere to be found. I sat in the silence. I prayed. I meditated. I slept. I walked. I went to Mass. At dinner I could see the other retreatants' experiences of God on their faces. I was jealous and heartbroken. I didn't think I could endure anymore.

On the last day of the retreat, I sat alone and humbled in my room. I wrote in my journal: "Lord, I am so restless today! It's hard for me to be still *or* quiet. Is it because I don't hear Your voice or feel

Your presence in the silence? I feel *so alone*. In some strange way it feels worse than alone. How can I be content in a place where I'm so miserable? Where the One thing I want I don't seem to have? (I know, Lord!)

"As I wait for my tulips to bloom, I wonder if they might not: not enough water, too much water, too cold. Maybe I didn't plant them deep enough, or maybe I planted them too deep. There are a thousand reasons why they might not bloom! Then I wonder if I might rot in my hole like my tulips could. I feel helpless, Lord! Totally dependent on You for my care. So why do I worry? I trust You completely for that care, and You alone know what I need. While I might kill my tulips, You will never let me die in my dark, empty, lonely hole. Please keep nourishing me even when I can't feel Your presence; even when I can't hear Your voice; even when I can't see Your face.

"I am helpless, Lord. I can't do anything by my own strength — I don't have any. I depend on You for everything. I have no control over my days, but You know what they hold. Help me to give up whatever control I thought I had. Help me to accept whatever my days bring as a gift from You. Help me respond to the circumstances of those days in a way that brings You honor and glory. Help me to let go of anything that keeps me from You. Help me to love You with everything that is in me. Help me to love others as You would have me love them. Help me to be only what You want me to be. Help me to decrease so that You might increase. Help me to wait for Your perfect timing—even when I want so badly to be out of the dark. And help me to be quiet so I can hear Your voice when You do speak to me."

CHAPTER 28

For Me To Live Is Christ

"CONTENTMENT IN THIS DARK HOLE. Peace in the midst of chaos. Joy in the midst of trials. Music in the midst of noise. Burning love in the midst of apathy. Hope in the midst of despair. Trust in the midst of confusion. May my life be a reflection of You." This became my prayer. Instead of focusing my attention on how I felt, I determined to live the way God wants me to live. I would try to keep my focus on Him and on other people. I determined to live the Gospel values the best I knew how. I would remain faithful to my Savior. I didn't understand what He was doing, but I had new confidence that He knew — that He had a plan. So I would learn to live in this darkness — my entire life if necessary; I would learn not only to be content in the darkness, but to enjoy it, to rejoice in it.

Could I learn to love God with my whole heart, mind, and soul even if I received nothing in return? Could I love God for Who He is and nothing else?

Could I be joyful even in these circumstances? These were my goals. Learning to enjoy this gift of darkness was like learning to love misery and hardship. I could see being content there, but joyful? My prayer became, "Lord, this joy will have to be a gift You give me; I can never get it on my own. Some days I can be content, but I'm dependent on You for even this."

I had a burning desire, an itchiness, to get on with my life after treatments ended. There were a couple of weeks that I felt pretty good—really good, actually—and I jumped back into my before-cancer activities with enthusiasm. It felt as if I finally had my life back! It felt so *good*! I had an intense desire to live every minute to its absolute fullest, and resting on the sofa just hadn't felt like "living" to me. So I returned to my choir. I started my piano lessons in addition to the organ lessons I'd begun during chemo. I worked in the food pantry. I went out for lunch with my girls and my friends. I started house projects. I wore myself out.

I started sleeping twelve hours every night and dragging myself through my days. My doctor told me to clear the calendar for two months and *relax*. Oh—so hard for me to do! But I cleared the calendar of everything but choir and organ lesson, delegated the food pantry work again, put the piano lessons on hold, cut way back on my out-and-about activities with friends. I might as well have cut off my arm. I felt helpless and frustrated.

But as I started to slow down, I began to realize that I had been feeling a tug-of-war between doing what I wanted/needed to do and quieter more enjoyable pursuits. It feels so selfish to spend time doing things I enjoy, but altogether wonderful! And maybe I could even enjoy cooking again if I could slow down and not be rushed. My approach to my diet and other health-building activities had also been causing me stress. Could I find a more relaxed way to take care of my body without it consuming so much of my time and energy? And the most important question of all: Could I learn to treat myself gently? That may not be the question everyone needs to ask herself, but I tend to tackle life with possibly more enthusiasm than is necessary. Learning to be gentle with myself, learning to give in to my physical need for rest, learning to give in to my need for quiet and down-time: these do not come naturally or easily to me. But I had come to the point that my body was so worn out I had no choice but to give in to it.

I began to spend more time at church practicing the organ. Being alone in the dimly-lit church playing hymns connected me to God's peace and settled my soul. I also started spending more time in the Adoration Chapel, just sitting quietly with my Savior. I didn't have much to say to Him, but it was comforting to be there. And I was able to spend a week completely alone in a little cabin on the edge of a pasture. In another time I might have thought I couldn't be so removed from my normal life, but that week was a joy and a blessing and came to an end all too soon. That rest was what I needed, for my body, my mind, my spirit.

As I started slowing down, my mind had more time to "be" with God. I began to understand that whatever was happening while I was in that dark hole was His doing, not mine. As I began to be still, to be focused on God, He began revealing Himself to me, speaking to me again. "In Mass yesterday I had a glimmer of love for Your people. It wasn't that burning love you showed me months ago, but it was a peaceful, contented love swirling around me. Maybe there is hope that I will be in the sunshine soon. I'm so grateful for even that small sign of hope" (Journal entry). God had let me see just a tiny part of Himself, but to a person who had had nothing of Him in months, that tiny part felt like the world!

CHAPTER 29

Speak Lord in the Stillness

S EVERAL WEEKS AGO, I had planned on dropping
in on the neighborhood ladies' Bible study,
but God had different plans for me that morning. I
felt that He was calling me to be with Him in the
Adoration Chapel at our church. I sat there for a
while, wondering what it was that I was supposed
to be doing. I had tried to pray, but that didn't feel
right to me; so I just sat quietly, waiting for Him to
show me what He wanted me to see. He brought my
soaring dream back to me, so vivid I could again feel
the wind and the sunshine, the peace, the joy, the
freedom. As I soared I became aware of my arms
stretched wide like the eagles' wings; then I realized
that my arms were stretched out like Christ's arms
had been on the Cross. In a flash the experience
ended. I felt certain that God was showing me that
there was a connection between soaring and suffering, but that connection seemed elusive. Like the

wind and the sunshine, I knew it was there, but I couldn't quite grasp it.

I decided to go to my concordance and find every Bible verse I could about eagles and soaring. Maybe they could give me a broader picture of what it meant to soar. Like a mind map, each reference gave me new words and ideas to explore.

I started in the book of Exodus (19:4) where God said to the Israelites: "I bore you up on eagle wings and brought you here to myself." Then came Isaiah 40:31: "They that hope in the Lord will renew their strength, they will soar as with eagles' wings; they will run and not grow weary, walk and not grow faint." Enthusiasm took over as I explored what God meant when He said He "bore you up on eagle wings." My word search took me to "sustain," to "provide for." Psalm 55:23 says, "Cast your care upon the Lord, who will give you support." I was beginning to get a picture of what soaring could mean: being brought new strength, new energy, new perseverance, new provision. So maybe as I soared in my suffering, as I gave that suffering back to God as a sacrifice of praise, He used it to provide for my needs and to bring me into a deeper relationship with Him. The passage in Isaiah promises strength, energy, perseverance — all things I desperately need, but how do I get them? The first part of that passage gives me the answer: "Wait for the Lord." As I tried to figure out how to do that, I began to think about all the times things weren't happening on my time table; all the times I wanted to (or did) jump in and try to take care of something instead of letting God work out the details; all the times I wanted answers *now*. Strength and energy and perseverance are all things I desperately need, but I won't get them by my own efforts; they are gifts God gives me when I let *Him* take care of the circumstances of my days, the circumstances of my life.

I continued my search by looking up verses that speak of strength. There are many, but they all convey the same thought: our strength *is* the Lord and is *from* the Lord. When I look to myself for strength, all I find is a fragile, weak human being, but when I acknowledge that fragility and weakness and give it to God, He gives me strength for the day, whether it's an "easy" day or a day of great suffering.

Psalm 91:3-4 says, "God...will shelter you with pinions, spread wings that you may take refuge." When life throws us curve balls — and it always does eventually — our safe place, our refuge, is with the Creator of the universe, our heavenly Father. He is the only person bigger than the circumstances of our lives, powerful enough to either change those circumstances or to protect us in the midst of them.

And finally, Colossians (1:9-11) tells us that we are strengthened for a purpose, for attaining steadfastness and patience. God gives me strength, energy, perseverance, provision, a place of refuge, all for the purpose of attaining steadfastness and patience. And the end result is *hope* (Romans 5:3-5).

I was beginning to feel like I might be coming out of my dark hole. I was beginning to hear God speak to me again. I was beginning to feel His presence again. Words cannot describe the deep, deep peace, the joy, the complete happiness that brought me.

One weekend when we were snowed in and couldn't get to Mass, I was praying the Our Father and had the briefest glimpse of heaven: the Lamb was on the throne; all the angels and saints were worshiping; brilliant light—very diffused, misty light. I was in the throng singing, "Holy, Holy, Holy." And then it was gone. But I opened my missal for my daily Scripture readings and read: "Faith makes us taste in advance the light of the beatific vision, the goal of our journey here below. Then we shall see God 'face-to-face' 'as He is.' So faith is already the beginning of eternal life"[4] (see also 1 Corinthians 13:12). Oh…I think the sun is shining!!

So…I've learned that there are times God reveals Himself to us and times He chooses to conceal Himself from us. There are times God speaks to us and times He chooses to be silent. We cannot understand these movements of God; His ways are far above our ways (Isaiah 55:8). But how we respond to the suffering, the hardships, even the ordinariness

---

4   *Catechism of the Catholic Church*, n. 163.

of life is up to us: we can either "draw near to God" (James 4:8) or we can turn away from Him. When we choose to draw near, He blesses us beyond our comprehension. His mercy, His compassion, His forgiveness, His eternal love are waiting to be poured out upon us in superabundant measure. His gifts of peace and joy, even in the midst — especially in the midst — of suffering are there for the asking. He's offering; He's just waiting for us to accept them. God longs to meet us in the suffering of life, not to remove it, but to be there with us in it. He longs to be the One we turn to when we need the comfort of a friend. He longs to be our Everything.

CHAPTER 30

Spirit of God, Descend Upon My Heart

"*F*IDELITY IN THE MIDST OF ARIDITY proves that we are seeking God and not merely our own satisfaction."[5]

During my "dark days," I felt like I was floundering, like there was nothing for me to hold on to. Without the awareness of God's presence, how could I know with certainty that I was still growing in my relationship with Him? As I often do, I turned to my priest for guidance. He assured me that God was still very present and explained that God can work in our souls in ways that are beyond our perception. He told me that I need to be looking at my actions for proof of growing prayer: Was I remaining faithful to Mass attendance, prayer, adoration of Christ, generosity, morality? That faithfulness was the indication of Christ's presence in my soul. He

....

5   Thomas Dubay, *Fire Within: St. Teresa of Avila, St. John of the Cross, and the Gospel-on Prayer* (San Francisco, CA: Ignatius Press, 1989), 222.

helped me to see that there is a kind of prayer that goes beyond words and thoughts and even listening. It's the "being" that God has been teaching me; it's a "deep-in-the-soul" kind of prayer that defies human understanding. God is using this darkness to purify me, to draw me closer to Him, to unite me to Him in a deeper, more precious way. This intense longing for God—even when it feels one-sided—is a form of prayer where words and thoughts are not only unnecessary, they hinder the work God is doing. It took a while for me to grasp the enormity of that, but I finally had something concrete to measure my progress or lack of progress by! I had been looking to my feelings for reassurance of God's presence within me, when I should have been looking for the fruit of that presence: "…love, joy, peace, patience, kindness, generosity, faithfulness, gentleness, self-control" (Galatians 5:22). My focus should have been on Christ, my Savior, not on my feelings. I knew better!

What I needed to learn was to want what God wants, to accept the circumstances of my life, to accept my suffering as Christ accepted the Cross: with complete trust in the Father, with complete humility, with complete love. I needed to learn to let Him live His life through me. I needed to learn to love my neighbor. "If we love one another, God remains in us, and his love is brought to perfection in us" (1 John 4:12). "This is the way we may know that we are in union with him: whoever claims to abide in him ought to live [just] as he lived" (1 John 2:5-6). What a standard! But I have to remember my "try harder" lessons and ask God to do it for me, because by myself I know it's not possible.

My highest priority has to be to "seek first the kingdom [of God] and his righteousness..." (Matthew 6:33). Everything else will fall into place if my priority remains what it should be. How do I do that? Every thought, action, and word need to please God. Being more concerned for others' needs than my own pleases Him. For me that translates into caring for my husband, our elderly parents, our children, and grandchildren. It means investing time and money in the food pantry. It means being available to a friend who needs to talk. It means that the people God has placed—and will place—in my life are very important. How I interact with them could make all the difference to them—and to me. God can use me in the briefest encounter. A smile can turn someone's day (sometimes someone's life) around. A helping hand makes a person feel less alone. A listening ear can give them hope. We never know how God will use us to reach another person. I need to be very aware of that as I live my days. Is all of this seeking God and His righteousness? I think it is because that is my proper response to God's love for me: love Him and love my neighbor. And "neighbor" is whoever I come in contact with today. It doesn't replace time with God in His Word and in prayer, but it is an extension of it. It is the result of it. So while I have a plan for my days, I need to stay flexible and open to the opportunities God sends; I need to see interruptions and crises as God's plan overriding my own and not let them upset me. And I need to let God's peace and joy and love pour through me to everyone my life touches. I may be the only Christ they ever see!

CHAPTER 31

Holy, Holy, Holy

HERE IS NOTHING LIKE facing death to make us ask the *big* question: Why am I here? A few weeks ago, I spent an afternoon in an old country cemetery. The sky was clear, the air was crisp, the ground was soggy from heavy rainfall earlier in the week. I was completely alone, with nothing to hurry me along. As I looked at the headstones — many from the 1800s — I began to wonder what those peoples' stories had been. Had they come here from another country? Did they eke out a living farming this hilly land? Were they neighbors who gathered together to worship, to share a meal? Were they happy here? It dawned on me that everyone has a story, everyone has a history and circumstances that make us unique. We are just specks of dust in the whole scheme of history, and yet God loves us so much that He made each of our lives unique and special. Part of learning to "love our neighbor" is to learn their stories: What are their joys, their hardships, their unique experiences? When we are interested in their lives, they feel God's love through us, and only God knows how that can affect all eternity.

But back to the cemetery. I began to notice the graves of so many babies and children. They were on this earth for such a short time—some born and died on the same day. What was their purpose? Why did God create them if they weren't going to "accomplish" anything while they were here. I stood there looking at those old, crumbling headstones, pondering that question for much of the afternoon. And while the answer wasn't new to me, it really hit me hard that we were created for eternal life with God, the Creator of the universe; He made us to be His children, to spend all of eternity praising His Holy Name. He made us for a relationship with Him that our human relationships can only hint at.

While God invites us into this beautiful relationship and gives us the grace we need to respond to that invitation, He also gives us free will and will never force it on us. When we become the willing participant in this joyous mystery, in His Fatherhood, He then gives us more grace to grow in that relationship with Him. We're to seek first His kingdom, love Him and love our neighbor, seek forgiveness for our sins, pray without ceasing. He gives us the grace to do these things He asks of us. We still must do them, but it is only by being open to and receiving those graces that we are able. So it becomes a beautiful circle: God sends His grace, we accept it to do what He asks of us, and when we do those things we open ourselves to receive more graces from Him. So the circle continues to widen and we gain more capacity to be filled with Him. And that is a deeply compelling, beautiful place to be.

That's what these final thoughts are about, as I struggle with the issue of what my "new life" — after cancer, after resting — will look like. I certainly don't have all the answers, but I can share my struggles and my thoughts, and hope that in some way God will use them to encourage you in yours. As I add activities back into my days, I need to remember to ask God what activities *He* wants me to participate in. (You have to remember that I'm the "go-getter"; I want to do it *all!*) I need to remember that I don't need to be doing "big" things for God — just doing the small daily things in a way that shows His love. When I die, my greatest wish is that people will say they saw God in me. And that will be enough.

I'm anxious to pack as much living into my days as I can. But only the Lord knows how many I have and what He wants me to do with them. Sometimes I wonder if this eagerness "to get on with it" is fear. I think I want to do *everything* today because I don't know if there will be a tomorrow. Am I still holding tight to life as I want it to be, instead of letting go of it and waiting for God to give me the life *He* wants me to have? Help me find a balance, Lord. "Teach us to count our days aright, that we may gain wisdom of heart" (Psalm 90:12).

Help me love You minute by minute as I live my days. Help me do what You want me to do. Help me be what You want me to be. Whatever activities I add to my days, I know that my highest priority is lengthy periods of silence with my Savior. I need to allow plenty of time for reading, writing, prayer, music, family, and friends. I need to include a lot of "down time" in my calendar. I need to allow for as much sleep as I seem to need. I need to eat well without making myself crazy in the process. I need to take a short walk every day. I think I need to only do the administrative part of the food pantry and let the volunteers handle the day-to-day work. (I have a really hard time with this one because I *love* working in the food pantry!) I need to only do what I have the energy for — and lately that's not much!

CHAPTER 32

Abide With Me

*W*HEN I FIRST LEARNED of my cancer diagnosis, I found that I needed huge chunks of time alone with God. My spirit needed to bond with His Spirit. There was obviously nothing I could do to accomplish it; it was the work of the Holy Spirit. But I had to be open to that bonding. I had to be the willing recipient of His work; I had to be quiet so He could accomplish that work. Sometime during that process I saw a beautiful illustration of two chunks of wax melted together and then hardened. Not only can they not be separated into the original two pieces, but they become a new piece of wax that blends the unique qualities of the original pieces. Like the wax, I trust that Christ's Spirit has become mingled with my spirit in a beautiful bonding that cannot be separated (see Romans 8:38-39). It is this new life – a depth of life I never knew was available to me (to all of us) – that I'd like to share.

Everything that I am belongs to God: every deed, every word, every thought, every breath. As I learn to live post-cancer, post-resting, and pre-whatever-is-next, He is using every moment of every day to draw me closer still to Himself and to mold me into the person He created me to be. He grinds off the rough edges, buffs and polishes until one day I will be perfect and holy as He is perfect and holy. (I have no illusions here: I have a very long way to go!) These are often not pleasant experiences, but if I can learn to cooperate with, instead of fighting against them, they will be completed sooner and with less pain. This is a hard, hard lesson for me to learn and an even harder one to put into practice.

This state of being melded into Christ's Spirit, of facing life's challenges with joy in the personal knowledge of His amazing grace, is a beautiful place to be. I'm not going to pretend that life is easier because of it, but nothing easily gained is valuable. Yet it's that peace and joy in spite of hardship that becomes the center of my life. It all becomes a prayer—whether verbalized or beyond words—that is offered up to our Savior for His praise and glory. Every thought is thanking Him, petitioning Him, praising Him. Every breath is from Him and for Him. Every day is a gift to be lived for Him. He is my everything. So even when I am not actively praying, my soul is always praying. Prayer has become my life, but hopefully, my life has become a prayer offered up to God continuously.

What exactly does this "oneness," this abiding with Christ look like? The Psalmist tells us that those who "walk without blame," "doing what is right," "speaking truth from the heart" (Psalm 15:1-5), abide in the Lord's tent. The New Testament tells us that if we keep His commandments (1 John 3:24), don't sin (1 John 3:6), live as Christ lived (1 John 2:6), love our brother (1 John 2:10), "eats my flesh and drinks my blood remains in me and I in him" (John 6:56), then we are abiding in Christ. How can I possibly "live [just] as he lived"? (1 John 2:6). I am a weak, frail, sinful human being incapable of those very things God asks of me. I don't have a solution, but thankfully God provides the solution for me. When I open my heart and invite the Holy Spirit to dwell within me, then He does the work. And when we're so bonded with Him, then we open the door for Him to do them in us and through us. What an amazing accomplishment! What we can't do for ourselves, He does for us.

John 6:56 tells us, "Whoever eats my flesh and drinks my blood remains in me and I in him." How can we possibly eat His flesh and drink His blood? If this is such a necessary part of abiding, there must be a way for us to do that. And once again Christ provides the way through the Church He instituted over two thousand years ago. When His anointed priests consecrate the bread and wine during the Mass, His Spirit comes upon them and they "become for us the Body and Blood of our Lord" (Eucharistic Prayer). What a beautiful and priceless gift! Every time I go to Mass and "eat His flesh and drink His blood" (1 Corinthians 11:26), that ball of wax becomes more Him and less me. He fills my being with Himself (after all, we "become what we eat!"); He replaces me with Him. John 6:63 goes on to say, "It is the Spirit that gives life.... The words I have spoken to you are spirit and life." And it's this life — the very life of Christ — that I get to live today. Whether I live it here on earth or eternally in heaven, it's the same life, life given to me by my heavenly Father, the great God of the universe, the Creator of all things. It's the life spoken of in 1 Peter 1:13, "So set your hopes completely on the grace to be brought to you at the revelation of Jesus Christ." It's the only thing that matters.

A few weeks ago, the Scripture reading for Mass was "Blessed are you who are poor, the kingdom of God is yours.... But woe to you who are rich, for you have received your consolation" (Luke 6:20, 24). I've always wondered about those verses because, obviously, if we compare ourselves to most of the world, we Americans are rich indeed. Scripture points out many dangers of having earthly riches, and yet King David lived in great wealth and still God called him "a man after his own heart" (1 Samuel 13:14). So simply having riches doesn't seem to be the problem; it just makes it very easy to have the problem. One priest said it well: "Ultimately, the reason the poor are blessed is that they have no worldly attachments to keep them from God. In their poverty, they have to trust God completely. Having no earthly goods, they are more inclined to seek the goods of heaven and thus are greatly blessed" (Father Jason Tyler, February 13-14, 2010). The light turned on! It's about being detached from the things of this world. It's being indifferent to our circumstances. It's about desiring only God Himself. It's not about not having things, it's about Who we look to for all of our needs and desires. Maybe this is what the darkness was about. God wanted me to desire only Him so He could bless me beyond my imagination. He wanted to give me the best there is: the gift of Himself.

CHAPTER 33

All That Thrills My Soul Is Jesus

Y DOCTOR HAD WARNED ME that the anniversary dates of finding the lump, being diagnosed with cancer, and surgery often bring depression: from the loss of control of so many aspects of my life, from so many changes to my body and mind, from so many uncertainties of what the future might bring. But instead of depression, the Easter anniversary brought me overwhelming joy. Joy to be alive, certainly, but joy in being fully alive in Christ has no comparison. The weeks of Lent were ones of recognizing God's great love for me; the cost of saving my life was unimaginable suffering—Christ's suffering on the Cross. I took a long, hard look at that suffering, and what I saw is love beyond my comprehension. There is nothing I could possibly do to pay that price myself, and I'm simply not capable of that kind of self-sacrificing love. But it brings me face-to-face with my sin, my human limitations, my enormous need for my Savior. Every time I enter our church, the crucifix above the altar reminds me of that sacrificial love. Every time I enter the church, I am brought to my knees in humble adoration of a Savior who loves me so much.

On Easter Sunday the altar was decorated with white lilies and yellow tulips. Now I'm sure no one bought those tulips with me in mind, but God surely planned them for me. Blooming tulips had become my promise of hope that God would bring me into His sunshine, that I would again experience the joy of His presence. But they also represent new life: the life God has given me after cancer, after the darkness; the life of abiding deep in His Spirit; the life that follows death on earth—life I was given a glimpse of and a yearning for during my treatments. Those tulips are the symbol of the fulfillment of God's promise of that life. I don't fully understand their significance, but my soul surely does.

There is nothing else like the Easter celebration in a Catholic Church. There is no need to convince anyone of Christ's Resurrection; it is simply the joyful, exuberant celebration of that fact. We belong to a very large, multi-cultural parish, and as the music, the languages, the customs of those cultures come together in one joyous celebration, I am reminded once again that it's not just "our church," "our language," "our culture"; it is God's Church in the world, without limits on time and space. It is the Church we will experience in heaven.

As God pours out His love and mercy on us during these next Sundays of Easter, I pray that His love, His mercy, His grace will flow through me to the people around me. I pray that they may see Christ in me in a new, compelling way. I pray that I am willing to be used by Him in whatever way He chooses, be it in health or sickness or even death. He gave His life for me; now I give my life fully to Him.

CHAPTER 34

How Great Thou Art

A FEW MONTHS AFTER OUR CONVERSION, my husband and I went on a pilgrimage with other members of our parish. We got to visit several Catholic churches built by German immigrants at the end of the nineteenth century. The artistry in those sacred buildings is breath-taking: stained glass, hand-painted murals, mosaic, gold leaf, sculptures, carved woodwork—and the organs! (One had hand-painted pipes; oh, it was beautiful. I could almost hear the music played on it throughout the decades.) All those artists had left their marks on this world—something tangible of themselves for those of us who followed to experience. These churches are hidden treasures, there for anyone who wants to see them, yet ignored by most. But for those who are willing to take the time to visit them, the effect is profound.

Having a deep, abiding relationship with our Lord is very much like that artwork: it is there for anyone to experience, but most will pass it up in the busyness of life, not even aware of the treasures they are missing. Many will pass it by simply because no one ever told them about it! It makes me wonder how many people in my life don't know they can have such a beautiful, deep relationship with Christ, or about the truth and beauty of the Catholic Church, or about prayer so deep that it defies human experience because I haven't told them. These gifts that God so freely gives are available to all who seek, to all who respond to His heavenly invitation to life in Him, to all who are willing to surrender their very lives to Him. It becomes a life full of peace and joy that defies description, a life of love beyond our understanding, a life of hope that carries us through the roughest storms. But until we take the time and steps necessary to experience these joys for ourselves, they will never be ours. Anyone who has them knows that they are worth every sacrifice, every letting go, every giving up. But no one else can do it for us. We must take that first step. If we do, we will be eternally grateful.

Our pilgrimage left one other lingering question: What will I leave behind for others to see and experience and remember when I'm no longer on this earth? What thing of beauty will others touch and see after I'm gone that will change them? Encourage them? Spur them on to their own experience with God? The beauty of this question is that I don't have to discover its answer. If I spend my days discovering and doing what God wills for me, then He will answer the question. He will take my days and use them in a way that only He can design.

And so my journey has come full circle. Six years after leaving our old church and life behind us, God has given me a deeper understanding of what it means "to be," to rest in Him. He has given me new understanding of "Be still and know that I am God" (Psalm 46:11). He has used the trials of life to bring me to a deeper, more peaceful, more joyful place in Him, where I'm able to face life with complete trust in my Lord, with fearless following of my Savior, with new hope for eternal life in heaven with my loving heavenly Father.

I pray that God will give all of us the grace to let Him mold us into the beautiful pieces of art that He created us to be. I pray that we will accept His gifts of mercy, love, and compassion that He wants to pour out upon us and the hope that only He can offer. And I pray that we will spend eternity praising our Savior together.

> *"So let us confidently approach the throne of grace to receive mercy and to find grace for timely help."*
>
> *Hebrews 4:16*

About Leonine Publishers

Leonine Publishers LLC makes fine Catholic literature available to Catholics throughout the English-speaking world. Leonine Publishers offers an innovative "hybrid" approach to book publication that helps authors as well as readers. Please visit our web site at www.leoninepublishers.com to learn more about us. Browse our online bookstore to find more solid Catholic titles to uplift, challenge, and inspire.

Our patron and namesake is Pope Leo XIII, a prudent, yet uncompromising pope during the stormy years at the close of the 19th century. Please join us as we ask his intercession for our family of readers and authors.

Do you have a book inside you? Visit our web site today. Leonine Publishers accepts manuscripts from Catholic authors like you. If your book is selected for publication, you will have an active part in the production process. This book is an example of our growing selection of literature for the busy Catholic reader of the 21st century.

www.leoninepublishers.com